WHAT BINDS MARRIAGE FOREVER

What Binds Marriage Forever

Ida Friederike Görres

Translated by Jennifer S. Bryson
Introduction by Jonathan Bieler

The Catholic University of America Press
Washington, D.C.

The paper used in this publication meets the minimum requirements of American National Standards for Information Science—Permanence of Paper for Printed Library Materials, ANSI Z39.48-1992.

Cataloging-in-Publication Data is available from the Library of Congress

ISBN: 978-0-8132-4039-8 (paper)
ISBN: 978-0-8132-4040-4 (ebook)

Book design by Burt&Burt
Interior set in Meta Serif Pro, Meta Sans, Super Clarendon

CONTENTS

This book is a translation of Görres, Ida Friederike. *Was Ehe auf immer bindet: Unsystematische Meditation zur Unlösbarkeit der Ehe, anthropologisch betrachtet.* Ehe in Geschichte und Gegenwart, 1. Edited by Wilhelm Arnold, Hermann Conrad, and Hubert Jedin. Morus Verlag, 1971.

The first epigraph for this translation (x) is from the essay "Our Image of Christ," first published in German in 1968. In Görres, Ida Friederike. *Bread Grows in Winter.* Translated by Jennifer S. Bryson. Ignatius Press, 2025.

The second epigraph for this translation (xi) is from Görres, Ida Friederike. "Geleitwort" (translated by Bryson). In Thomas Gilby, *Kleiner Kompaß für Eheleute,* 7. Verlag Herder, 1956. [The original English edition of Gilby's book was published as T. G. Wayne, OP. *Morals and Marriage.* Longmans, Green and Co., 1936.]

Dedication for the German edition of *What Binds Marriage Forever* (1971)

*Dedicated to those who fought for Creed and marriage at the Synod of Wurzburg in January 1971. In memory of my wife, who has gone home [to the Lord].**

According to Francis de Sales, it often happens that two upstanding people, who both have good intentions but different views, contradict each other vigorously and increase each other's burdens. With this in mind, my dedication applies to all who fight righteously in the Way of our Lord. This includes when we need to differentiate our position clearly from those of others.

CARL-JOSEF GÖRRES
(1905–1973, husband of Ida Görres)
August 21, 1971**

* Regarding the connections between the Synod of Wurzburg, the death of Ida Görres, and those who "contradict," "increase each other's burdens," and "fight righteously," as Carl-Josef Görres writes, see Jennifer S. Bryson, "The Death of Ida Görres during the Synod of Würzburg & How Pieper Learned of It from Ratzinger."

** Carl-Josef Görres appears to be paraphrasing from Francis de Sales, *An Introduction to the Devout Life*, 124–125 (Part III, Chapter 3).

Dedication for this English translation

Dedicated to those who, through their fidelity to their marriage vows, through thick and thin, bear witness to God's fidelity.

JENNIFER S. BRYSON
Lincoln, Nebraska
Feast of St. Michael the Archangel, 2024

He is the center of their existence; they measure everything they do and do not do by His Word and Will by its effect for His Kingdom. . . . I think of the unhappy ones who do not divorce because of this, of the divorced who forego a second marriage to someone newly discovered—staggering testimonies that He is Lord.

IDA FRIEDERIKE GÖRRES
1968

"Walnut of Eden" by Vladimir Kush (b. 1965), © Vladimir Kush

With each passing day, the conversation about marriage grows in gravity and urgency. For centuries, this important part of human life was deeply and, it seemed, inextricably embedded in a complex, far-reaching structure of the ties as well as traditions of clan, nation, law, economy, and religion. Like a nut in its shell, the married couple's relationship with each other rested within something, it was "elevated," sometimes in a double sense of this word. This protective and supportive housing of the past has long since been broken open and the interior stands naked in an environment that has changed.

IDA FRIEDERIKE GÖRRES

1956

INTRODUCTION

Jonathan Bieler

Today, the term *marriage* is fraught with such varied, disputed meanings, and the Catholic teaching on it is so little understood, that the present new English translation of the book *What Binds Marriage Forever* by Ida Friederike Görres will undoubtedly prove to be a contribution to help readers grasp the rational and human quality of the Catholic concept of marriage and grapple with the modern charges brought against it. The book *What Binds Marriage Forever* was the last publication of Ida Friederike Görres (1901–1971); she sent the manuscript to the publisher eight days before her death on May 15, 1971.[1] Görres, deeply learned in

1 The day before her death, on May 14, 1971, Görres collapsed after addressing a meeting of the Synod of Wurzburg (1971–75) held at the Jesuit and Diocesan Seminary of St. Georgen in Frankfurt, Germany. Bishop Hermann Volk had nominated Görres to attend the Synod, which was a series of meetings of bishops, clerics, and lay people in Germany, gathered by the German Bishops' Conference to find ways to implement the decisions made at the Second Vatican Council. She died the following day of a cerebral hemorrhage at a hospital in Frankfurt. See Hanna-Barbara Gerl-Falkovitz, "Zur Einstimmung," 15. (An English translation of *Von Ehe und von Einsamkeit*, including Gerl-Falkovitz's entire "Zur Einstimmung" essay, is forthcoming in

Church history, sheds light on the historical roots and context of marriage and brings this into a discussion with the contemporary notions of marriage, always with an eye to real-life people and their oftentimes complex situations. Her unique style of writing is steeped in insights closely derived from her own concrete experience serving in the Church, such as her work with girls and women, and displays her education as well as her poetic skill.

Someone, it is not clear who, asked her to write on the topic of the indissolubility of marriage. We read in a letter Görres wrote on May 11, 1971, to Father Paulus Gordan, OSB (her last letter to him before her death on May 15), "And so, the last few weeks I have been downright frantically busy. The article I was requested to write last July on the indissolubility of marriage has swelled to a treatise of 60, sixty pages to be exact. I sent it the day before yesterday, a load of bricks off my shoulders."[2] It was an era of growing controversy in the Church over marriage, and Pope Paul VI's 1968 encyclical *Humanae vitae* loomed large in the background, as it was heavily criticized by many in the German Church for its insistence on the inseparability of the unitive and procreative significance of marital

Ida Friederike Görres, *On Marriage and on Being Single*.) See also Bryson, "The Death of Ida Görres during the Synod of Würzburg & How Pieper Learned of It from Ratzinger."

2 Ida Friederike Görres, *"Wirklich die neue Phönixgestalt?"*, 494.

love—while Görres, by contrast, praised the encyclical as "prophetic."[3]

In *What Binds Marriage Forever,* she criticizes the view that marriage is founded *exclusively* on the personal, mutual, and affective love of the spouses. She concludes that the spouses' emotional love cannot serve as the sole basis for the indissoluble union the Church considers marriage to be. In other, more systematic words: the unitive aspect of the marital act is by itself not enough to serve as the stable ground of the sacramental form of marriage in the Church, nor as the ground for familial and civilizational stability, whether inside or outside the Church.

It is in light of this debate on the foundations of marriage that her concerns about what binds marriage forever can be understood. Görres first identifies the obstacles in the Church and society that prevent an acknowledgment of the interconnectedness of all the aspects of marriage. By looking at history, she gains a deeper sense of the traditional role and purpose of marriage as *generation* in the double sense of lineage and procreation. Then Görres considers the three authoritative factors that bind marriage forever: covenant, law, and grace—that is, sacrament. Hence, the title of the book: *What Binds Marriage Forever.* Strangely enough for modern ears, upholding the Church's teaching as authoritative allows Görres to highlight, rather than disregard, the crucial role of human activity and

3 Ida Friederike Görres, "Trusting the Church: A Lecture" in *Bread Grows in Winter.*

responsibility in marriage. Love or, as the case may be, tensions are often a fruit of conscious actions, even though these actions may seem insignificant and involuntary. As she observed in her journals in the 1940s, "And love arguably only grows, when we exercise and strain it, not by preserving it and saving it for special occasions like a good dress."[4] In other words, love is something living, not a dead possession.

Görres brings to light the depth of the Church's understanding of marriage in a way that often rings strange to the modern reader who is more accustomed to political rather than sacramental thinking. At least since the beginning of the twentieth century, Western nations' legal frameworks increasingly did not leave room anymore for sacramental realities, such as the indelible character of baptism, the sacramental mark of priestly ordination, and the indissoluble bond of marriage. One sees this, for example, in the work of the early twentieth-century Austrian legal scholar Joseph Unger (1828–1913), who argues for the legal capacity of "fallen" priests and monks to be civilly married.[5] In her book, Görres criticizes that the Church's hierarchy of her time made it easy for fallen priests and religious to be married in the Church with all honors after renouncing

4 Ida Friederike Görres, *Nocturnen*, 199.

5 See Joseph Unger, *Priesterehen und Mönchsehen*, 9. For the state, as Unger argues, the impediment to be married is an impediment related to the class or the profession of a certain class of people in the state. He then says: "It thus follows by logical necessity that upon leaving the clerical state, the impediment to marriage based on this is removed." ("Daraus folgt mit logischer Notwendigkeit, dass mit dem Austritt aus dem geistlichen Stand das daran geknüpfte Ehehindernis hinwegfällt.")

their religious state of life.[6] She shows, thus, that many theologians even within the Church viewed marriage more through the eyes of the political state's legal framework than from a sacramental vantage point.

In 1964 and 1965, when she published two essays about problematic aspects of marriages between Catholics and non-Catholics, the push to expand allowing such marriages was a hot topic.[7] In *What Binds Marriage Forever*, we see how, just a few years later, the debates had moved further along to the question of allowing divorce and remarriage for Catholics. Several times, Görres quotes an article from 1970 by Robert Hotz, SJ, from the Swiss Jesuit journal *Orientierung* (*Orientation*), in which he argues for allowing Catholics to divorce and remarry.[8] The passages Görres quotes from Hotz show that for an increasing number of their contemporary Catholics (at least in German-speaking Europe), the sacramental logic of marriage as an objective, real, and indissoluble bond was itself the very scandal, as it would, they alleged, cause suffering by hindering divorced Catholics from remarrying and by excluding remarried Catholics from participation in the sacrament of the Eucharist at Mass. Görres was anything but indifferent to the struggle, suffering, and sacrifice

6 See, for example, Sections 5, 63, and 80.

7 Ida Friederike Görres, "Einige Überlegungen zur Mischehe" 1964, and "Die Mischehe: Erwägungen über einige Grundlagen ihrer Neuordnung," 1965. She republished both in her book *Be-Denkliches*, 1966. The quotations from these essays in this introduction are from unpublished translations of the essays into English by Jennifer S. Bryson.

8 Hotz, "Wiederverheiratung Geschiedener in der Kirche?" 211–19.

involved in the Church's high standard for marriage. In this book as well as her 1949 book *On Marriage and on Being Single*, Görres shows far-reaching tenderness and awareness for this very suffering of people in broken situations. Not only that, but through her careful analysis and account of what leads to these situations, she resists a simple identification with the suffering and cheap accommodation for their situations out of a disposition of "inverted envy," which she diagnoses in the Church, using a phrase coined by her brother Richard Coudenhove-Kalergi, as a premature readiness to give up one's own gifts and position for the sake of the suffering and underprivileged partner in dialogue, so as to remove any whiff of superiority or authority.[9] Görres, herself a noble countess by birth, a child of the imperial and royal Austrian diplomat Heinrich von Coudenhove-Kalergi and his Japanese wife, Mitsuko Aoyama,[10] was well aware of this human disposition she found in the Church and society in general, and the way it subverts from the very outset any positive and fruitful sense of hierarchy and tradition. For Görres, however, true human compassion with those who suffer, and true and good authority, always go together.

Görres's compassion with the human situation and her trust in the authority of the Church's teaching spring from a single source: her faith in God, in whom mercy and justice are but two forms of one and the same love

9 See Section 10.

10 Regarding Görres's parents, see Anna Findl-Ludescher, *Stützen kann nur, was widersteht*, 47–53.

for humankind. From the same source, she can also hold together the sacramental and gracious reality of the marriage bond with the sometimes complicated, even messy, human freedom and activity within the objective form of this very relationship, as Görres says in *On Marriage and on Being Single*:

> What good fortune that in this it does not depend only on our running the race, rather on God's grace—like the old image of the indispensable work of the farmer, which nevertheless depends entirely on the favor of the weather. Christian marriage takes place in the Church, which is a place of grace. Christian marriage symbolizes the unique, never-ending, immeasurable fruitful marriage of Christ with the Church. This statement is not just edifying and "poetic"; it is serious and means something real: namely that what takes place in the vast and mysterious exchange of lives actually enters into a discrete marriage that is integrated into the Church.[11]

Faith in God and sacramental realities allow Görres to hold together the aspects of marriage that she deems to be lost in a one-sided emphasis on affective love as the only foundation of marriage: alongside the unitive aspect, the Church teaches that the sacramental aspect of marriage as well as the procreative dimension are essential. This means that we do not understand the affective aspect of love, unless we situate it within

11 Görres, *On Marriage and on Being Single.*

the other two, the sacramental and the procreative. This was the very point of Pope Paul VI's encyclical *Humanae vitae*. For Görres, Hotz's argument that marriage is indissoluble only as long as it is constituted by personal, affective love and his conclusion that a marriage is dead and already dissolved unless this love is present bespeaks an overexaggerated equation of a certain type of love and marriage, one that Joseph Ratzinger already saw developing in the writings of Herbert Doms at the beginning of the twentieth century.[12] Görres turns Hotz's argument upside down by concluding that marital love as an expression of God's covenantal love for Creation is not the root but the fruit of marriage, a result of a conscious vow to enter into this covenantal, objective, and real relationship and be freely obedient to it to the end. "Love," writes Görres in this book, "can find its place within *fides* and *sacramentum*; it is very much desired. Yet love is not its root, rather its fruit."[13] Or as she phrased it in her 1964 essay on mixed marriages, "What is desired and expected is love from marriage—not marriage from love—i.e., conjugal affection, deep and sustainable, which should grow out of faithful life together."[14]

Embedding love into the context of free obedience to a covenantal love allows Görres to give human freedom and sovereignty of the self a more prominent

12 Joseph Ratzinger, "Zur Theologie der Ehe," 4:565–92.

13 Section 23.

14 Ida Friederike Görres, "Mixed-Marriage: Considerations on Some Basic Principles for Reassessing Mixed-Marriage."

place than it is given in what she calls the determinism of the circumstances from which human erotic love results. The question is: What moves me to enter into marriage, and what moves me to leave a marriage? For Görres, the Catholic understanding of self-mastery or self-possession that is fulfilled in a sincere gift of self (*Gaudium et spes* 24) is more proper to the rational and volitional nature of humans than the alternative idea of delivering the form of one's life up to the fickle moods of erotic love, to which the loving relationship of two persons tends if it excludes its relation to family, society, and religion. She is well aware of the scandalous ring her remarks have for people of modern times, who hold this purely mutual love, whether fleeting or as "couple-marriage" or "private marriage," as she calls it in her 1965 essay on mixed-marriage,[15] as the highest value. At the same time, Görres is also critical in her essays of kinship-marriage, if the marriage is entered into for purely financial or political reasons. We can only gather that for Görres, these are not truly free and human acts of consent that constitute a properly Christian marital covenant.

What binds marriage is not simply the result of passionate forces or certain interests. What binds marriage is the covenant. Görres asserts this point succinctly in her short essay "Marriage: This Is a Great Mystery" from 1966.[16] As Görres discusses in this essay

15 Görres calls "couple-marriage" and "private marriage" *Paarehe* and *Privatehe*, respectively. See Görres, "Mixed-Marriage."

16 Görres, "Marriage: This Is a Great Mystery."

and Bryson explains in her preface, the German word for covenant, *Bund*, is related to the verb to bind, *binden*. And as Görres explains, "A covenant is established, it is concluded. Something occurs with will and deliberation: it does not just 'happen'; a covenant is an act and an action."[17]

This covenant that is not so much produced but entered into as an objective form that constitutes the basis for the sacramental marriage; it is that which binds. This marriage is a new and real thing, a flesh, one body, that is more than the consent of the spouses but embodies their union and may not simply be taken back at will. Görres compares the marriage to the objective reality of a child, who cannot simply be "declared nonexistent" when the mutual consent to have a child ceases.[18]

In this book, Görres's method is to place marital love within a wider "anthropological" context.[19] She draws on the key tenet of Aristotelian anthropology that man is a social animal and refers to the social human reality of this using the Latin word *gens*, which she equates with the German word *Geschlecht* in the sense of "the connected sequence of generations from a point of origin." The *Geschlecht* or *gens* is kinship,

17 Görres, "Marriage: This Is a Great Mystery."

18 Görres, "Marriage: This Is a Great Mystery."

19 The full subtitle of *What Binds Marriage Forever* in the original German edition is "Unsystematic Reflection on the Indissolubility of Marriage, Considered Anthropologically." Given the extensive length of Görres's subtitle, The Catholic University of America Press has chosen to omit it in this English edition.

that is, the generation, the larger multigenerational family, the dynasty, or the lineage—the social reality that lies between the human species in general and the individual. She calls this form of marriage the *Geschlechterehe* or *gens-Ehe*, translated in this book as "lineage-marriage" and "kinship-marriage," respectively (see Translator's Preface).

In the preface Görres wrote for the 1956 German edition of *Morals and Marriage* by Thomas Gilby Wayne, OP, which is quoted in the epigraph the translator added for this English edition, Görres uses the image of a nutshell to describe the way the *gens* served as a protective layer around a marriage. She writes, "Like a nut in its shell, the married couple's relationship with each other rested in something"; today, however, "this protective and supporting housing of the past has long since been broken open and the core stands naked in a changed environment."[20]

The *gens* is constituted by the connected succession of at least three generations from a single origin and as such is deeply bound up with fruitfulness, with procreation, as the condition for this handing on of life, including land and power, from generation to generation. Thus, the double sense of generation is held together in the reality of the *gens*. Marriage is the single constitutive origin and connecting link of the generations within this line of familial succession. "The dominant reality," says Görres in her diaries in the 1950s, "is the blood—the *gens*, the clan; 'generation' in

20 Görres, "Marriage in a Nutshell—or Not."

this wide comprehensive sense—pertaining not to *Eros* but, if you like, to *pietas*."[21]

Historically, she argues, marriage has been seen entirely within this context and still is in cultures different from Western culture. This is why the purely erotic love of individuals, their exclusively *personal* bond formed at the expense of the continuance of the family, long had the odor of taboo and scandal, as it would likely lead to chaos and tragedy in the form of the dying out of a lineage. According to Görres, the Church took up and validated this anthropological reality of the *gens*-marriage, but also, as it were, baptized *gens*-marriage by additionally emphasizing to the same degree the free and intentional loving and personal bond of the spouses over against a pure obedience and submission to the will of the clan. To be sure, this is a delicate balance between *eros* and *pietas*, and Görres argues that such a balance is held only within the Church. Only a sacramental marriage is able to prevent the scales from tipping either toward the imbalance of a pure *gens*-marriage or toward marriage as an exclusively personal attachment between uprooted and self-sufficient individuals for the sake of their private happiness.[22]

21 Ida Friederike Görres, *Broken Lights*, 206. Of course, the classic example of *pietas* is Virgil's Aeneas, who gives due honor to the gods, his family, and the state.

22 See Görres, *Broken Lights*, 207. Note: on page 207, the translator of *Broken Lights* omitted this short paragraph on the modern individualistic view of marriage that appears in the German edition; see Ida Friederike Görres, *Zwischen den Zeiten*, 280. See also Görres, *Nocturnen*, 151: "On

To be sure, in the Church, the balance is real: marital love is, for Görres, entirely personal and mutual, even erotic, while at the same time it is in its essence related to the seriousness of fruitfulness and the lifelong commitment in generating a family and handing on the faith to one's children and grandchildren. In that view, the child as the fruit of the marriage is essentially related to the union of the spouses that is a generative and generational reality because the child is more than a biological product, rather a successor, a carrier of what has been handed to the spouses and what they have to pass on to the offspring.[23] Görres says:

> Physical union is reserved for marriage [. . .] because marriage is *essentially* wedded to fruitfulness [. . .] procreation being a sacred, momentous, highly responsible charge, which calls for a mode of life fully adapted to it—which is exactly what marriage is intended to be [. . . . M]arriage is the sanctuary of those lovers who may—and must—undertake the great venture together of bearing fruit, each to each.[24]

For Görres, the order and reality of marriage can only be understood with a view to the interconnectedness of its unitive, procreative, and sacramental aspects. Absolutizing any one aspect means losing

---

the other hand, it is the very signature of our time, that the human being is being uprooted down to the last fiber."

23 Görres, "Mixed-Marriage."

24 Görres, *Broken Lights*, 46.

sight of the complete form of marriage and, ultimately, reducing the human being and his or her freedom.

For Görres, true compassion for human brokenness cannot simply consist in disregarding the entire sacramental form of marriage, as that would come at the price of losing its very intelligibility as the sign and image of our covenantal relation to God Himself, who in complete freedom entered into this covenant and asks for our yes to it. From this, it becomes clear why adultery was the sign par excellence by which the prophet Hosea publicly displayed Israel's sin, as marriage between man and woman is a reflection of God's very relation to the human being.[25] God wishes for our consent to His covenant, and marriage allows as well as takes completely seriously this consent in its objective reality that transcends the moment. What is more, consecrated virginity in the Church is, for Görres, the ultimate expression of the eschatological reality of the human being's spousal and fruitful relation, that is, freely marrying God Himself. By losing sight of the essential dimension of fruitfulness in marriage, Görres argues, we also lose sight of what the virginal state of life in the Church means in the first place: "We have no true mystique of virginity, for the very simple reason that we have no mystique of marriage, i.e., love lived as unity *and* fruitfulness. [. . .] Virginity as the mystery of *divine marriage*:[26] love in oneness and fruit-

25 Görres, *Broken Lights*, 9.

26 The word that Waldstein-Wartenburg translates here as "divine"—*übernatürlich*—means, literally, "supernatural." Görres, *Broken Lights*, 111, and Görres, *Zwischen den Zeiten*, 151.

fulness *in ordine religionis*."[27] Marriage and virginity are what allow the human being to truly receive this supernatural life.

Görres is aware that erotic love must be understood in its connection to fruitfulness in order to be valued and safeguarded for its own sake. If erotic love is absolutized—that is, pursued only for its own sake—at the expense of the potential fruit it generates (by intentionally preventing such fruitfulness), the fact of nature that erotic love tends to fulfillment in the fruit that wants to be borne is negated. By intentionally, actively denying, as a matter of principle, that one of sexual desire's goals is fruitfulness of some kind, one hollows out its very essence.

Perhaps a reason for the profound power of sexual desire lies in the human desire for one's own life to continue in another person and thus in generations—in the *gens*. One might even go further and say that sexual desire is ultimately rooted in and derives its immense power from the natural desire for life or survival. Therefore, to let this desire be fruitful is the way in which my life keeps going, by passing it on to another—that is, to the child. By denying the desire its fruit, we declare this desire meaningless and thus evil. We might argue that at the heart of the modern cult of sexual desire lies a profound and desperate devaluation and misunderstanding of this very sexual desire and the human being as such. Or, in Görres's words, "Youth

27 Görres, *Broken Lights*, 110–11. "*In ordine religionis*" that is, in the order of religious life. Görres means a religious kind of fruitfulness, of which marriage is an image or symbol.

is in itself the *yet* unburdened state. . . . But to attempt to keep it forever only leads to sterility in every sense: monstrous perversion of youth, destined as a blossom of the fruit."[28] The value and identity of erotic love is not safeguarded in opposition to the fruitful life whence it springs and whither it leads. Görres says, "We must distinguish between flesh become transparent—and flesh set up as an idol."[29] Hence, Görres can say that the indissolubility of the lifelong commitment the spouses give to each other is not essentially placing a limitation on their freedom, even with its obligation to abstain from possibly even greater erotic union with other persons. Rather, marriage presents itself to us as something reasonable and good, as a form—a structure—for flourishing human personal love that is able to receive, care for, and hand on the gift of life throughout the generations—a life that is ultimately a free gift and that the Church orders under the blessing from God.

28 Görres, *Broken Lights*, 118.

29 Görres, *Broken Lights*, 112.

TRANSLATOR'S PREFACE

Jennifer S. Bryson

In 2019, when I first discovered Ida Friederike Görres and began translating her book *On Marriage and on Being Single* (1949), I wanted to read more of her works. After exhausting my searches among used booksellers in North America and Europe and buying several books, I explored eBay to see what else I might find. It was on eBay, of all places, that I came across the German edition of *What Binds Marriage Forever.* I had never heard of the book.

At that point, no online used bookseller in Europe or North America had even a single copy of *What Binds Marriage Forever* for sale. It had been out of print since first being published in 1971 and, at this time, remains out of print. In 2022, when I recommended the book to the librarian at Hochschule Heiligenkreuz in Austria, it took me several months of searching before I could find a used copy for him to purchase. Now, I am hopeful that the publication of this English translation of *What Binds Marriage Forever* will help return this insightful book to a status of more than something one might stumble upon on eBay.

Terminology: The Presence of Covenant in Bind and Bond

Covenant is a central concept in this book. However, the repeated significations of "covenant" in Görres's use of language are not as obvious in English as they are in German. To start with, the centrality of "covenant" is evident in the title of the book in German, *Was Ehe auf immer bindet*, in a way that is not obvious when this title is translated into English. In German, the verb *binden* is etymologically related to the German word for "covenant," *Bund*. In this way, the book's title, *What Binds Marriage Forever*, itself is already a gesture toward covenant. (I did not use the word "covenant" in the title because, in this context, the German verb *bindet* translates not only accurately but also most clearly and smoothly into English as *binds*.)

Additional indications of the centrality of "covenant" are scattered throughout the book. It will be helpful for the reader to bear in mind that, from Görres's perspective as a speaker of German, the concept of covenant is suggested, if not directly implied, in the verb *binden* which I translate in this volume as "to bind" and the noun *Bund*, which I translate as "bond" or "covenant," depending on context.

Terminology: Multiple Types of Marriage

In this book, Görres shows how "the word 'marriage,' which was still a clear concept yesterday, wavers and fluctuates elusively today."[1]

An unusual aspect of the language in *What Marriage Binds Forever* is Görres's use of distinct labels for different ways people understand this thing they all call "marriage." Some of these labels are neologisms Görres created to draw—indeed, to highlight—distinctions between different notions of marriage.

German, like English, has one main word for marriage: *Ehe*. With her multiple labels, Görres is trying to show that while everyone in society was using the same word "marriage," people were, in fact, using it in different ways. We continue to experience this today. She uses compound German words as labels to provide twenty distinct labels for nineteen different concepts of marriage (the first three are synonyms, as I explain below). I have translated these as follows.

SYNONYMS

1A. *gens-Ehe* kinship-marriage

1B. *Geschlechterehe* lineage-marriage

1C. *mehraltrige Ehe* multigenerational-marriage

1 Section 16.

INDIVIDUAL TERMS

2.	*Fürstenehe*	royal-marriage
3.	*Liebesehe*	love-marriage
4.	*Paarehe*	partner-marriage
5.	*Personehe*	marriage of individuals
6.	*Pflichtehe*	obligation-marriage
7.	"*Probe-Ehe*"	"trial-marriage"
8.	*Scheinehe*	sham-marriage
9.	*Sex-Ehe*	sex-marriage
10.	*Sklavenehe*	slave-marriage
11.	*Sippen-Ehe*	clan-marriage
12.	*Stammesehe*	tribal-marriage
13.	*Standesehe*	status-marriage
14.	*Suksessiv-Ehe*	serial-marriage[2]
15.	*Tier-"Ehe"*	animal-"marriage"
16.	*Vernunftehe*	accommodation-marriage
17.	*Versorgungsehe*	provision-marriage
18.	"*wilde Ehe*"	cohabitation-"marriage"[3]
19.	*Zweckehe*	convenience-marriage

2 Serial-marriage is the label Görres uses when describing the views of advocates for divorce and remarriage; Görres herself calls this "serial polygamy."

3 The German phrase *wilde Ehe*, literally "marriage in the wild," refers to a marriage (or "marriage") without religious or state sanction as a marriage. Common translations of *wilde Ehe* include cohabitation, common law marriage, and, less often, concubinage. I think "cohabitation" is closest to the meaning intended by Görres in this book.

Via the Index, readers who are interested may find her uses of these terms.

Görres does not articulate comprehensive definitions for each of these terms. Some, like kinship-marriage and lineage-marriage (synonyms), she discusses in depth. Others, such as status-marriage and provision-marriage, she mentions only in passing. This is one of the "unsystematic" aspects of this book, as articulated in the German subtitle of the book.

The first two terms on the list—kinship-marriage and lineage-marriage—are used interchangeably. In my estimation, the third, multigenerational-marriage (used only once and likely drawn from Rosenstock-Huesssy), is a synonym of the first two.

The translation of the synonyms *Gechlechterehe* and *gens-Ehe* warrants particular attention. I translate these as lineage-marriage and kinship-marriage, respectively. In this book, Görres uses kinship-marriage most frequently, ten times, as opposed to twice for lineage-marriage. I think the reason she has two labels for one concept is that she is replacing her use of lineage-marriage (*Geschlechterehe*) in her early works with kinship-marriage (*gens-Ehe*) in this book in 1971.

Today, the German word *Geschlecht* is usually translated as "gender," meaning sex (as in male or female) or gender (with its ever-expanding range of meanings). However, historically, including in Görres's lifetime, the word *Geschlecht* commonly also meant lineage, kinship group, line of descendants, or house in the sense of a noble family, as in "the House of Windsor." While these latter meanings can be found in the etymology of the English word "gender" in its Latin root *genus*, few English speakers associate these meanings with "gender" today. And likewise, ever fewer speakers of modern German associate *Geschlecht* with its historic use to mean "lineage" or "kinship."

Thus, I think a likely explanation for why Görres transitioned from exclusively using *Geschlechterehe* (lineage-marriage, that is, *Geschlecht* + *Ehe*) in an essay on marriage in 1965 to *gens-Ehe* (kinship-marriage) in most instances in this book in 1971, is that the meaning of the word *Geschlecht* changed rapidly and significantly in German (as did "gender" in English) between 1965 and 1971 as the sexual revolution accelerated.[4] As a result, for the sake of clarity, Görres replaced the German word *Geschlecht* she had used in 1965 with the less ambiguous, equivalent Latin word *gens* in 1971. From comparing her uses of these terms in her 1965 essay and her book in 1971, it is clear she intends the same meaning with both. Nevertheless, I translate *Geschlechterehe* and *gens-Ehe* differently—as lineage-marriage and kinship-marriage—to indicate to the reader that Görres is using different terms. The reader, however, will do well to keep in mind that lineage-marriage and kinship-marriage are synonyms.

Section Numbers

This book does not have chapters. Instead, it consists of separate, short reflections. In the original version

4 Görres, "Mixed-Marriage."

of this book, the reflections are separated only by an asterisk-like symbol. For this English edition, however, I added section numbers to the reflections to facilitate reference to them by those who might discuss or write about this book.

Register of Persons, Index of Biblical References, and Index

I added a Register of Persons, an Index of Biblical References, and an Index to this English edition. None of these are present in the German edition of 1971.

Görres is inconsistent in how she writes names in her texts, not only in this book but in other works as well. Sometimes, she mentions first and last names; other times, only last names; on rare occasion, such as "Thomas" for St. Thomas Aquinas, only first names. I have left this inconsistency of hers in the text. Where necessary to prevent confusion, I added additional information in brackets. Overall, where possible, I have identified these individuals in the Register of Persons. When information about a saint's life is directly relevant to a passage, I provide that information in a footnote. Otherwise, general information about the saints mentioned in this book will be found in the Register of Persons.

Citations

Except for the citations in Bieler's Introduction, and one in the body of the book (as noted), all the citations have been added by me.

A few times in *What Binds Marriage Forever*, Görres mentions the authors of her quotations in parenthetical remarks, but she usually provides no further information, such as title, date, or publication. In two cases, however, Görres mentions some of the details of a publication she quotes. I have left such information in the text as Görres had it, in parentheses.

The first time she provides source information in the text is for an article from 1970, "Remarriage in the Church for the Divorced?" ("Wiederverheiratung Geschiedener in der Kirche?") by the Swiss Jesuit Robert Hotz, SJ. While Görres is responding in *What Binds Marriage Forever* to an entire trend by Catholics of a certain theological orientation attempting to unravel the Catholic teaching on marriage, in this book, Hotz's article, which she calls "a kind of manifesto,"[5] serves as a precis of this trend. Thus, it plays an important role in this book, so she provides the title and date of publication. Fortunately, I was able to find the original article. In some of the citations, since English readers may not be able to read Hotz's article in German, I provide some context or additional information from Hotz's article about the passages to which Görres refers or which she quotes.

5 Section 12.

In the second instance where Görres provides source information, it is detailed information about a French work on canon law, perhaps because most German readers would unlikely have been familiar with this work in French.

Overall, however, the inconsistency and the incomplete nature of her source information tell us something about how she worked: she appears to have been quoting from memory sometimes—perhaps often. Perhaps she did not want to delay finishing the text since it was already longer than she had planned, and she was very busy with preparation for the Synod of Wurzburg (see Bieler's Introduction). Not least of all, as was her approach in her other books, she wrote for a broad audience and was thus more concerned with getting a message to her audience than with academic details. Her heart was always focused on (educated) Catholic readers at large, not academics.

I identify the sources of Görres's many quotations to the extent I was able to find them. Where applicable, I quote established English translations or the original English text of these quotations. When I could not find an established English translation, the translations of these quotations are my own. Wherever there is a quotation with no citation, it means I could not identify a source.

As for references from the Bible, only two times, namely when Görres quotes John 14:26 and Ezekiel 3:18–19, does she mention the source in parentheses. For consistency, I moved this information to the footnotes. Görres loved the Bible and knew it well. Her scattering of biblical references—taken for granted that they would be recognized without citations—is typical of her style.[6] To assist the reader, I have added citations for most of these references.

Orthography

When translating from German to English, the translator must make decisions not only about syntax and words but also about orthography. In German, all nouns are capitalized. Compared to this strict rule of German, English capitalization has significant flexibility, especially regarding religious terminology (for example, commandement or Commandment). In capitalizing names, titles, and pronouns for God as well as that which comes from God (for example, Creation, Revelation, Scripture), I allowed the thrust of Görres's work—namely, that this book is an expression of her Catholic faith—to serve as my guide. However, there is an exception: where I quote from primary sources, I have left the orthography in those quotes as it appeared in the printed text. One example of this is the quotations from the Bible, for which I use the *Revised Standard Version of the Bible: Catholic Edition* (RSVCE); the RSVCE does not capitalize the pronouns or titles of God or the word "church" (when referring to the Church), whereas, outside of quotations, I do.

6 See for example Ida Friederike Görres, *The Church in the Flesh*, including the Index of Biblical References I added to the English edition (233–236).

ACKNOWLEDGMENTS

I express my gratitude to Thomas D. Klingenstein, whose support helped to make this translation possible, to Hanna-Barbara Gerl-Falkovitz for her encouragement, to Hochschule Heiligenkreuz in Austria, where I was able to work on the citations for this translation while in residence as a Visiting Researcher, and to the helpful librarians of the joint libraries of Hochschule Heiligenkreuz and the Abbey of Heiligenkreuz. My appreciation is also due to Don Prudlo, whose unusual frankness and honesty in talking about the Catholic teaching on the indissolubility of marriage piqued my curiosity about the nature of marriage; this, alongside other factors, led me to want to learn more and, after I stumbled on this book on eBay, contributed to my willingness to translate this book. I thank Nathaniel Hurd for introducing me to Jonathan Bieler. Finally, I wish to thank the staff of The Catholic University of America Press for bringing this English edition to fruition and to Ann Aubrey Hanson for assisting.

WHAT BINDS MARRIAGE FOREVER

Marriage is the highest mystery. Marriage is, for us, a popularized secret. A pity that there is, for us, only a choice between marriage and solitude. Extreme it is—but how few people are capable of a genuine marriage—and how few can even endure solitude.[1]

NOVALIS

Rationalism is a certain abuse of Reason; that is, a use of it for purposes for which it never was intended and is unfitted. To rationalize in matters of Revelation is to make our reason the standard and measure of the doctrines revealed; to stipulate that those doctrines should be such as to carry with them their own justification; to reject them, if they come in collision with our existing opinions or habits of thought,

1 Novalis, *Pollen and Fragments*, 60. In this English version of this quotation, "mystery" and "secret" translate the same word, namely *Geheimnis*. An alternative translation could read, "Marriage is the highest mystery. Marriage is, for us, a popularized mystery." Note how Görres bookends *What Binds Marriage Forever*, opening and closing the book with an echo of Ephesians 5:32 here and in Section One, and then a quotation of it in the final sentence of the book. Also, in 1966, Görres used the first part of this verse as the title for an essay on marriage in 1966: Ida Friederike Görres, "This Is a Great Mystery."

or are with difficulty harmonized with our existing stock of knowledge. And thus a rationalistic spirit is the antagonist of Faith; for Faith is, in its very nature, the acceptance of what our reason cannot reach, simply and absolutely upon testimony.[2]

JOHN HENRY NEWMAN

1

It is with careful deliberation that I set forth the following statements from great thinkers. When those who challenge indissoluble marriage maintain that indissoluble marriage cannot be established compellingly and comprehensively by Scripture or Tradition, nor by law, nor through historical practice, we say calmly that they are correct. Not because of their arguments, which are often shallow and hang only by a thread, but because wanting to prove *everything* can provide only a sketch at best, leaving out the essentially mysterious character of marriage.[3] Again, the iceberg shows only its tip. Our consideration merely circles around it and tries to illuminate it from all sides. As for the rest of what marriage is, it makes itself known only to faith.

That is why what follows regarding an anthropological understanding of monogamy is meant merely to offer avenues of approach and aids to assess the situation.

2 John Henry Newman, "On the Introduction of Rationalistic Principles into Revealed Religion" (tract no. 73, *Ad Scholas*), 32.

3 See Ephesians 5:32 and footnote 1.

2

"Indissolubility of marriage" is now a central topic of discussion inside the Church. However, if we reach down critically to find the roots of this immense flood of discussion, it turns out that, in reality, the controversy is the opposite: it is the *solubility* of the marriage—but not even this, because separation after marriage as well is *not* a problem and in itself would be of interest only to a few. The real issue, instead, is the greatest possible *rehabilitation and permission* for the *second marriages of those who are divorced*, which, of course, cannot be defended and championed otherwise than through the proposition of the absolute solubility of marriage, even Christian marriage. This is what would have to be proven, not Church doctrine. The tremendous exertion and the fantastic outlay of intelligence that are used here expose the intensity of the emotional forces that have an interest in this.

3

This fight did not come out of nowhere. Somewhere, Kierkegaard speaks of the great temptation to "take the side of humans against God."[4]

4 Perhaps Görres is referring to this passage by Kierkegaard: "All this interpreting and interpreting and scholarly research and new scholarly research that is produced on the solemn and serious principle that it is in order to understand God's Word properly—look more closely and you will see that it is in order to defend oneself against God's Word." Soren Kierkegaard, *For Self-Examination: Judge for Yourself!*, 34.

4

This is a temptation for well-meaning hearts. The starting point in our question is clear and unavoidable: the situation of distress for the many thousands of divorced Christians, including "believers." The statistics paint a dismal picture. The divorce rates show an upward trend, and most divorced people are getting married again. In most countries, there is little difference among [Christian] confessions. Where there are still state barriers, as in Italy, socially accepted concubinage has flourished. Many Catholic Christians as well live in a situation of hardship or guilt. The priests, in particular, see the enormous extent of this and call out for help for those affected. Priests and laypeople, for example, demand that theologians seek and find defensible ways out. A way out of what? A way out of the distress of the remarried, to whom a Church wedding is denied, and of the divorced, on whom she imposes renunciation of new happiness in love. Both appear to be unbearable impositions. They argue: the claim of the Church to proclaim the Good News and to be the representative of the merciful God proves itself to be most outrageously unbelievable, as long as her law keeps these wounds open and insists on the concepts of guilt and restraint that society gave up long ago. If in any regard, it is here that adaptation to the times is in order.

5

This conflict is not confined to this topic; rather, it plays out in many concentric circles. The subject mentioned above—the right of the Christian, the believer, in some instances, to change partners legitimately, that is, the right to permissible serial polygamy[5] within the Church—may form the innermost core of the matter for many. If one asks about their *situation in life*, the response reveals an extensive web of intentions, aspirations, and connections. It reminds us of old battle formations: on a vast field, there is an intricate deployment in various lines, divided many times over into scouting parties, a vanguard, and skirmishers, into central columns with shock troops and siege devices, and into exterior flanks to secure the retreat.

The liberation of divorced spouses is at least subliminally part of the struggle for the liberation of the clergy from the duty of celibacy; the easier laicization of monks and nuns; the rehabilitation of homosexuals; unrestricted permission for birth control by all means, including abortion; as much approval as possible or at least trivialization of extramarital sexual relationships; and autonomy of conscience regarding sex before and within marriage. It is only logical as well as revealing that these "freedom fighters" also include in their battle cohort divorced people who are heavily burdened by current canon law.

5 In section 19, Görres refers to "serial polygamy" as "serial-marriage" when she is presenting how defenders of divorce and remarriage in the Church state their own arguments for this.

6

All these endeavors branch out from the same deep root: a particular idea of "happiness" as a state of wish fulfillment, predominantly in the erotic-sexual realm, to which [they say] every person has a birthright. Because this claim is expressly, generally, and specifically limited by commandments and laws, it results in a suspicious and aggressive posture of resistance to "law" in general.

The claims to happiness and *freedom* are almost always contiguous—indeed, at many points, they are related and they nourish each other. As a result, this may, in fact, be the root producing the general allergy to authority today in all forms that fall under the heading "repressive," such as the state and the family. Meanwhile, society, indifferent to religious and ethical norms, has already become broadly "permissive." Including the Church in the general hostility toward authorities is not only an "in addition," but an inevitable and specific insistence: not only does she, at least in principle, impose through her marriage laws and chastity requirement (which are closely related) the strongest still fairly effective barrier to lust, but she—as a troublemaker—even invokes divine, that is, absolute authority, while also appealing to divine mandate in her practical powers to bind and release. Anyone who wants to get past this successfully must strike far and deep.

7

This rebellious attitude is greatly reinforced by an, in and of itself, "innocent" element of the zeitgeist: the aversion to everything that stands firm. Religious laws have a long history; they are deposits from the lives of many generations. In a time of general flux, such as today, that which is long-lived and enduring is easily regarded from the outset as a burden, a barrier, a fetter, instead of, as until now, as protection, preservation, guarantee, rootedness, as the greatest earthly security of all which one person can give to another—and, moreover, as a reflection of God's immutability, a shadow of eternity on Earth.

8

(By the way, what does "until now" mean in this context? History repeats itself. In the period immediately after the French Revolution, which was also perceived as worldwide, irresistible change, Goethe wrote in *Elective Affinities*: "Anyone who knows how the world is must see that in marriage too it is only this settled everlastingness in a world of such mutability which is somewhat out of place."[6] This, sure enough, is how the adulterer argues.)

6 Johann Wolfgang von Goethe, *Elective Affinities*, 67. Another possible translation of the title of this book, *Die Wahlverwandtschaften*, is *Kindred by Choice*.

9

This skepticism against what is old, against what is unchanged, almost automatically includes intense belief in progress, which, on the one hand, considers the present as the "high point in time" to which everything previous adapts—or else should be destroyed. Second, everything emerging that is new, all that is "becoming," is perceived optimistically as the shortest path from better to best.

10

This pressure to change Church teaching and practice regarding marriage is reinforced by another very typical current of our times. We have often referred to this. It is the global power of *envy*, the power of those who are "underprivileged." This global power has succeeded in triggering a wave of guilty conscience as a response among those who feel that they are either better off in some way or who are merely viewed as such. Here, I have to agree with my brother Richard Coudenhove-Kalergi, who calls this attitude "inverted envy":[7]

7 Richard von Coudenhove-Kalergi wrote in 1921, "There is also inverted envy: that is what I call the distress of having more than others" (translation by Bryson). Richard Nicolaus Graf von Coudenhove-Kalergi, *Ethik und Hyperethik*, 20.

When Görres writes "I have to agree" regarding her brother Richard, she is drawing attention to a rarity. From her childhood until her death, she and her famous older brother Richard were nearly polar opposites in almost every regard, not least of all in the contrast between her Catholic faith and his lifelong contempt for religion, especially for Catholicism. As a child, he mocked his younger sisters for their piety (see, for example, Görres, *The*

The "fortunate person" identifies with the accusation of the accuser, agrees with him, no longer grants himself his privilege, and, yes, tries to partially abdicate himself and thus spontaneously satisfy the accuser's desire for leveling. It is the most peculiar mixture of justice and fear, suggestion and compliance, magnanimity and weakness, self-denial and feeling inferior! We encounter this in all possible relationships involving contrast that were formerly understood as opposites but are now declared adversaries: men and women, priests and laypeople, educated and uneducated, rich and poor, elderly and youth, normal and odd, empowered and as yet unempowered—who are joining together today to form new blocs of power.

People are now constructing a new "confrontational pairing" to add to these: those who are happily married versus those who have unhappily failed. People are trying to manipulate those of us who are happily married into having a guilty conscience, as if we, selfishly, as *beati possidentes* (those blessed to posses), defended a monopoly against our fellow unhappy humans. We should, so to speak, lay down the "crown" of exclusive legitimacy and voluntarily share this honor with the others:

> Jesus once said: "Let him who is without sin among you be the first to throw a stone at her."[8] Here, I would like to turn this into "Whoever of you live

---

Church in the Flesh, 97); later, he would become a Free Mason and ardent secularist.

8 John 8:7.

> in happy or tolerable marriages may well consider whether *you will not grant* to another, who has not been so fortunate, that the other too may live in peace."

That was in a sermon. What a subrogation![9]

11

This example of very skillful emotional propaganda (although its origins are innocuous) exemplifies the conscious tactics of those theologians who are engaged in this struggle. By the way, it is also important that theologians and priests, in particular, are the ones leading this. Today, there is a widespread view of the Church as *the* Establishment, the repressive and authoritarian power par excellence, and the clergy as her executive. This is why many of the members think they cannot rehabilitate themselves other than by proving that they are precisely *not* channels of oppression but are instead cutting-edge champions of liberation, by proving that they do not identify with the Great Usurper[10] of human happiness but with those oppressed by her. They are ashamed by a "collective guilt," and so the often-discussed trend to "make amends" also plays a role here.

9 The term translated as *subrogation* is *Unterschiebung*. This could also be translated as "transference of benefit." A subrogation is "the assumption by a third party (such as a second creditor or an insurance company) of another's legal right to collect a debt or damages." *Merriam-Webster Dictionary*, "subrogation," https://www.merriam-webster.com/dictionary/subrogation.

10 It is clear from the grammar of the German text that by "the Great Usurper" Görres means (ironically) the Church.

Once awakened in the Church, the will to reform is channeled all too far into this broad riverbed, where it mixes with completely different currents to a point beyond recognition.

12

In a kind of manifesto, those spearheading this fight explain with an openness that is either poignant or provocative:

> A change in previous practice cannot lie solely in legal changes that are enacted from above; it has to be a *slow but focused process* across the entire pastoral ministry in parishes. It has to have an influence on Christians and bring about a *change in their disposition toward belief.* Such a comprehensive and broad *reorientation* of pastoral care must prepare the *ground* for Christians to have a new understanding and new demeanor toward those who failed in marriage and remarried. In this way, the danger of a scandal, of the parish's resentment and indignation at a new pastoral approach, can be countered.
>
> (*Orientierung*, October 31, 1970)[11]

11 Hotz, "Wiederverheiratung Geschiedener in der Kirche?," 217. In English, the title of this article means, "Remarriage in the Church for the Divorced?" This essay from 1970 appeared in *Orientierung* (*Orientation*), a journal published from 1936 to 2009 by the Jesuits in Zurich, Switzerland.

13

So, "reprogramming the parish"? This means reprogramming the faithful, and this, in turn, means simply reprogramming the faith. This hits the nail on the head.

Because it cannot be said clearly enough: The indissolubility and solubility of marriage are not isolated propositions or principles. Both can only be explained and defended, and "they can only make sense," as the English language so aptly says, within a larger network of connections, from which many threads come together in this one node. So, is the indissolubility of marriage "inherent to the system"? Yes, even if this phrase ["inherent to the system"] is considered a curse word to others. One cannot understand the eye without reference to the face and the brain.

Christian marriage *grows out of* the context of the whole of faith—the Christian and Catholic image of God, Christ, the Church, and the human person. Christian marriage becomes uprooted when the background is faded or mutilated or when other forms are pushed quietly, almost imperceptibly, into its place until it hangs in the air, illogical and incomprehensible. The focal points at which these changes occur are as follows:

1. A change from Holy God—the Creator, the Judge, whose right to direct us humans, whose claim to our obedience is absolute, indisputable, and without which no hair falls from our head,[12] who

12 Luke 21:18.

commands His Will clearly[13]—into a "tame" God, indefinite, demystified, who commands nothing and forbids nothing that could stand in the way of our "happiness," a God whose only known quality is all-forgiving mercy, unconditionally. The expression, very questionable from the beginning, that humans are partners of God has had its creeping effect. After all, partnership always implies certain equality and equal rights.

II. A change from Christ, the Son of God, *Kyrios*, Lord of the Church, who has been present among His believers throughout history and still is today, from Christ who demands discipleship and carrying the Cross,[14] who spoke the terrifying expression about clawing out one's eyes and chopping off one's limb for salvation,[15] as well as about eternal life and remaining in His love by keeping His Commandments,[16] and about sending the disciples with representational authority to the end of time until He returns[17]—into a vague "historical Jesus," a Jewish do-gooder, of whom little is known but that He fought the Establishment of His time and fought for human rights, and who has left nothing behind other than an example that is difficult to interpret and texts of His disciples that are even harder to interpret.

13 See, for example, Psalm 19:7.

14 Luke 14:27; Matthew 16:24, 10:38.

15 Matthew 5:29, 18:9.

16 John 14:15.

17 Matthew 10:1–42; Mark 3:14, 6:7–13.

III. A change from the Church, His representative, the presence of the living Christ in Scripture, sacraments, grace, and also in the proclamation of His Commandments—into a mere organization, an earthly Leviathan, which hampers the "cause of Jesus" and must be dismantled and rebuilt all in His name, even more so in the name of alleged majorities for whom "democracy in the Church" means that the leadership exists to carry out the will of the people instead of divine authority.

IV. A change from people who are created to know God, to love, to serve Him through faithful work in His Creation, and to finally be saved forever—into people without an eschatological future, beholden to this one life and this one world, which attains its realization through the greatest possible happiness for the greatest possible number.

Into this framework, marriage which is soluble and repeatable as humans see fit not only fits seamlessly, but it grows out of it.

14

The indissolubility of *successful* marriage is not a problem for anyone. The most strident fighters spearheading legitimate, repeatable marriage are no less affirmative of this than the most obedient and pious. Those who live happily with one another do not need any philosophical, anthropological dissertations on the nature of person or love, nor laborious theological discussions about the sacramental nature of marriage. Certainly, these aspects are intrinsic to marriage, but they do not have to be conscious; a good couple can live together for a hundred years without having analyzed them or ever read a book about them. Whether the happiness of marriage means a fulfilling great passion—"But all joy wants eternity—Wants deep, wants deep eternity"[18]—or quietly satisfied comfort: "Do stay with me, you are so good,"[19] these couples would probably subscribe to Goethe's spirited apologetics expressed through the "intermediary" [a marriage facilitator] in *Elective Affinities*:

> Anyone who assaults the estate of matrimony . . . anyone who in word and worse in deed undermines that foundation of all moral order has me to deal with. . . . Marriage . . . must never be dissolved, for it brings so much happiness that in comparison any individual unhappiness is of no significance. And what do people mean when they speak of unhappiness? It is impatience, which comes over them from time to time, and then they are pleased to call themselves unhappy. Only let the moment pass and you will think yourselves fortunate that something which has stood so long still stands. There is never a sufficient reason for separation. The human condition is so rich in joy and sorrow that it cannot be calculated what a man and wife owe one another. The debt is infinite and can only

18 Friedrich Nietzsche, *Thus Spoke Zarathustra*, 227–28.

19 Johann Wolfgang von Goethe. *Faust*, 40.

be paid through eternity. It may not always be easy, that I do not doubt, and why should it be? Are we not also married to our consciences, which we should also be glad to be rid of often enough, since they are more difficult than ever a man or woman might be to us?[20]

15

When marriages become unhappy, when living together becomes torture, *separating* from a shared living space as a way out is still taken for granted. The problem being fought over with such passion arises only when a possibility for a *new* liaison opens up on the horizon. Only then does the question of commitment to duration become toxic, and today this is with two propositions: 1. A broken marriage is no longer a marriage; 2. Maybe it was not one from the start.

16

Now, which *basic concept* of marriage we are actually talking about is revealed. Because here, too, saying yes or no is not dependent on an isolated formation of opinion on one point; over the long run, it is anchored in the roots of the will. This is why people can talk past each other fruitlessly for hours if they want to pursue purely factual apologetics of an abstract

20 Goethe, *Elective Affinities*, 64–65.

"indissolubility." Instead, it is about the fact that the word "marriage," which was still a clear concept yesterday, wavers and fluctuates elusively today.

17

What one must decide, is this: Is marriage something *objective*, which binds the partners, something they enter into, an arrangement and way of life, to which they submit, whose inherent laws they recognize, which forms a "state of life" ("the honorable state of Holy Matrimony" says the Anglican wedding rite)? Or is it a *purely private* matter, identical to the subjective relationship of the couple to each other—this means it is determined uniquely, as a one-off, by this specific pair; its content is "love" (we must put this in quotation marks due to the ambiguity of the word) and "happiness." Both are purely subjective, predominantly psychological states of mind and, therefore, only the partners themselves would be capable of making, and in a position to make, statements about whether they exist and to make decisions about their duration.

18

Anyone who understands marriage as the *lifelong bond* of two people, as a fellowship of destiny, knows or should know that all possible difficulties and crises have been factored in from the start. As the wedding liturgy acknowledges: "for better and for worse, in health and sickness,"—the English formula adds explicitly: "in poverty and in wealth." And as the folk song expresses even better and deeper:

> Then come the wild weather,
> come sleet or come snow,
> We will stand by each other;
> however it blow.
> Oppression, and sickness,
> and sorrow, and pain,
> Shall be to our true love
> as links to the chain.[21]

—a confirmation and deepening, not grounds for dissolution.

19

The defenders of serial-marriage argue quite logically: Marriage is the *love*-bond of the couple. Love is constitutive for marriage in a large, deep, exhaustive sense, the full mutual gift of body and soul, total surrender, a total fusion of two people: no longer two, but one. The bond *arises* from *this* love; this love bears it. This love obviously demands unconditional fidelity and prevents adultery and divorce. This love reflects and manifests Christ's redeeming love for His Church and is represented in the earthly image. [As Hotz argues,] "Love is a mingling of two personalities. The

21 Anonymous, "Annie of Tharaw," in *Poems from the German*, 149. This version was translated by Henry Wadsworth Longfellow. An alternative translation of the last line quoted here could be, "Should be what ties our love in a knot."

indissolubility of marriage is a *consequence* of marital love. Marriage is indissoluble *insofar as* it is constituted by love."[22]

But: love is fleeting—who does not know this? So, [according to Hotz,] if love dies, there is no need for further fidelity. When love withers, the fidelity inherent only in it also withers away. "Marriage" then ceases to exist, and the nonexistent can neither be broken nor divorced, neither dissolved nor annulled. People become as internally free as before. When a new "love" takes hold of them, they are free to conclude the bond of love again.

To designate something else as a "covenant" or consisting of a covenant is, [in Hotz's view,] an "arbitrary hypostasis that is alien to reality, a mere fiction."[23]

20

Some theologians (because, it must be said right away, mainly theologians speak so unrealistically) want to find these views confirmed by the [Second Vatican] Council itself:

> The intimate partnership of married life and love has been established by the Creator and qualified by His laws, and *is rooted in* the conjugal covenant of irrevocable personal consent. Hence, by that human act whereby spouses mutually bestow and accept each other a relationship arises which by

22 Hotz, "Wiederverheiratung Geschiedener in der Kirche?," 213.

23 Hotz, "Wiederverheiratung Geschiedener in der Kirche?," 214.

> divine will . . . is a lasting one. As a mutual gift of two persons, *this* intimate union . . . impose[s] total fidelity on the spouses and argue[s] for an unbreakable oneness between them(*). Christ the Lord abundantly blessed this many-faceted love. . . . He abides with them [the spouses] thereafter so that just as He loved the Church and handed Himself over on her behalf(**).[24]

21

Lutheran Protestant theologians have long taken the same line: "The traditional concept of purpose must be *entirely* kept away from the understanding of marriage *as* a personal community of love" (Wendland).[25] There is awareness of the novelty of these representations. Bernhard Haring comments,

> The explicit emphasis on love as belonging to the nature of marriage was recorded here (in the Council decree) as elsewhere, despite those "modi" [suggested changes or corrections to drafts] that claimed that this preeminent role of love *contradicted earlier* documents of the Magisterium and

24 Vatican Council. 1965. *Pastoral Constitution on the Church in the Modern World: Gaudium et Spes*, Paragraph 48. Italics added by Görres. Gaudium et Spes cites (*) Sirach 17:3-10 and (**) 1 Corinthians 6:13-20.

25 Heinz-Dietrich Wendland, "Zur Theologie der Sexualität und der Ehe," in *Theologie der Ehe*, ed. Gerhard Krems and Reinhard Mann, 120.

gave the impression that the marriage could be dissolved as soon as love is extinguished.[26]

[Or as Hotz asserts,] "The consent always demanded by the Church is understood *as* an *act of love* in which the spouses give and accept each other."[27]

22

This all sounds impressive and moving, wonderful and grand. Nevertheless, the admonishers at the Council had a finer instinct. Joseph Ratzinger's remark, in his important essay "Zur Theologie der Ehe" ("On the Theology of Marriage"), is very interesting (though the essay nevertheless seems to me to warrant critical amendments in many ways): "The African bishops found the philosophy of love at the Council beautiful, but as the theology of *marriag*e, it was *incomprehensible and unrealistic* to them. It was interesting, of course, that the theologians who had helped provide this breakthrough were unable to deal with this problem. Basically, they were only able to say that everywhere one had to advance to the *level of our development* in which the true nature of marriage had been revealed."[28]

26 Quoted in Hotz, "Wiederverheiratung Geschiedener in der Kirche?," 216. The footnote for this quote in *Orientierung* (page 216, footnote 19) appears to include a citation of the source. However, in the pdf of *Orientierung* that I (translator) was able to access, this footnote is partially cut off and thus illegible.

27 Hotz, "Wiederverheiratung Geschiedener in der Kirche?," 216–17.

28 Ratzinger, "Zur Theologie der Ehe," 585. Italics added by Görres. Translation by Bryson.

The whole passage is extremely important. Here we are close to the core of the problem. The African bishops are there, unconsciously, as representatives of a consensus, which encompasses the entire history of humankind (*Menschheit*) on almost the entire globe.

This core problem lies in the modern, in my view unsustainably far exaggerated, *equating of marriage and love*—an attempt to cut through an immensely complex knot with a Gordian sword stroke.

23

Humankind has always known tension in the relationship between marriage and love and tried to handle it in different ways. But trying to identify them as one and the same is untenable. Even the most basic justice regarding our forefathers and regarding non-European cultures (not only the African ones) demands thinking through the phenomenon factually and impartially. Because according to this criterion, the overwhelming majority of all marriages up to our present day, including all Christendom in the past, would *not have been marriages at all.*

Who does not know that throughout history, at all levels of culture, from the highest of the Egyptians, Chinese, and Indians to tribes in which prehistoric conditions live on, in paganism, Judaism, Islam, Buddhism, in Christian society into our century, marriages were entered into and lived out for notably clear purposes and objectives that had very little to do with love. Its purpose was—and still is in some societies (East Asia,

Africa)—*generation*: in its twofold and very precise sense—the generations, namely those who are to come, and through generation as an act. Because marriage is understood to be *multigenerational* and not single-generational (Rosenstock-Huessy).[29] "Love" is neither its constitutive element, nor do the couple's essential ties derive from it. The constitutive element of marriage is what our moral theology called until yesterday the "goods" of marriage—*proles, fides, sacramentum*, namely, children, committed lifelong community, and inviolability of the sacred covenant. Love can find its place within *fides* and *sacramentum*; it is very much desired. Yet, love is not its root, rather its fruit.

Exactly this seems almost immoral to many contemporaries. They are embarrassed that the Church has supported this barbaric, as they see it, inhuman concept of marriage with her theology and practice for so long. Was not this concept of marriage a Moloch to whom the person was cynically sacrificed? Was not this Moloch (even apart from actual abuses, as when people were slaughtered for material assets, such as property and status) an abstract concept of "nature" and "species" that degraded marriage into a tool for "reproduction"? [Ratzinger writes,] "Its moralistic element was not taken from the personal and social element, *not at all* from

29 Rosenstock-Huessy addresses the difference between a multigenerational (*mehraltrig*) mindset and an individualistic mindset focused only on one's own, single generation (*einaltrig*) in several of his works. However, it appears that Görres's subsequent reference to Rosenstock-Huessy in section 26 is to his book *Soziologie*. Here, she may be referring to this passage: "Thus, marriage is an extension of time into the future of the human race," from Eugen Rosenstock-Huessy, *Soziologie*, 1:254. Translation by Bryson.

the anthropological, but ultimately from *the animal realm.*"[30] "The moral criterion of sexuality is that it happens 'naturally,' that is, 'sufficient for nature's sense of species.'"[31] This deserves a very critical look.

24

Has a couple ever joined together in life to "preserve the species, to save humankind from extinction"?[32] And, on top of this, out of obedience to professors of scholasticism or even to Church Fathers, such as Augustine? Do you really believe theological theories and abstractions have such an influence on real life? I do not.

It is very strange that moral theologians today, with incomprehensible ignorance, overlook the *crucial intermediate determination* that lies between the species and the individual: *kinship* (*gens*) and *lineage* (*Geschlecht*), not in the sense of sex but rather in the connected sequence of generations from a point of origin. The actual process in life of kinship is growth, maintenance, endurance over time. This requires three groups: the ancestors, the current bearers, and the descendants for whom the "heritage"—tangible

30 Ratzinger, "Zur Theologie der Ehe," 579.

31 Ratzinger, "Zur Theologie der Ehe," 579.

32 Görres is paraphrasing a passage in which Ratzinger discusses the view of some that "sexuality is a matter of 'nature'." He writes that according to this view, "it belongs to humans not as individuals but as a species; marriage, consequently, appears to be a function of the species and finds its essential meaning in its preservation." Ratzinger, "Zur Theologie der Ehe," 578.

as well as spiritual—is guarded and extended. This process is a unity: the handing over, the transmission, and the tradition as an object and as a perpetual act. Since humans are mortal, the actual bridges that keep passing on the legacy beyond the boundary of death are *marriages*. They are the guarantor of the temporal immortality of kinship. Whatever else brings the sexes together—looking for a love partner, and so forth—will be integrated within and subordinated to this primary task. By whom? Of course, by the elders, the parents who are responsible for the whole. Kinship determines the marriage; the young couple completes it. Marriage does not create a family; instead, it continues one. Clans form confederations (alliances, one still says in certain circles); the youth embody them.

25

The notion of multigenerational-marriage is not possible without powerful, if not yet reflexively systematized, ideas of death, duration, and preservation as well as goods that are worth preserving. The relationship to the future on which everything is based is *eminently human*. It is strange that today's worshipers of the future have become so oddly blind to this.

In marriage, the "child" is neither a more or less welcome "biological by-product," an occupational accident of eroticism, nor a "baby,"[33] an object of play and fondling in need of tenderness. The fact that the

33 In the German text, Görres uses the English word *baby*.

understanding of this could have slid down to this level is a most shameful testimony. Children are simply *that which is to come*, the future in person, for which all present achievements are done. No plans, structures, or institutions can realize the "future"; only living people who will replace us—and they simply have to be conceived and born, even if it is in the nightmare of genetics laboratories.[34]

Animals are acquainted with packs and flocks, not generations.

26

The couple and the covenant are, to a certain extent, only the raw material of marriages. It is also the case that the mental and bodily mating instincts are, on their own, unstable and unreliable. Couples search for each other, find each other, and separate from each other in infinite alternation. The couple needs the *covenant* to carry out the mission of kinship. This, too, is a specifically human element. There are also pairs among animals, as the zoologists and animal behavioral researchers describe for us tirelessly (sometimes not entirely untendentiously). They are tender, affectionate, engaged in a process of familiarization that is like a prototype of fidelity, even in exclusivity and staying together beyond the care of their brood. However, only humans can form a covenant that connotes knowledge

34 Görres considered artificial reproduction a profound horror. See, for example, Ida Friederike Görres, "Überlegungen zur künstlichen Menschenerzeugung."

of death, the future, and responsibility. The most primitive form of tribal-marriage already demonstrates this.

27

And what about love?

This is the great challenge with kinship-marriage. First, because, as I said, it is based on planning, that is, foresight and calculation. It requires early bonding and cannot wait for the more or less accidental encounter of two mature people. Rather, the freedom to choose a partner usually must be significantly restricted, based on screening considerations, such as the ability to marry and being on par with each other, that is, worthy and fit for their kin and their future. The scope for spontaneous erotic attraction is, therefore, very limited. Because family lineages are not built on what is by its nature the most unpredictable and volatile thing. The idea of falling in love *in advance* is missing. Falling in love—that is, erotic fine-tuning—should be encouraged during the engagement period. The clichéd sentence of Old Icelandic sagas, "and after the wedding, their hearts inclined toward each other," was probably true in many cases. Love should emerge from marriage, not the other way around. But love in the sense of the great eros-passion, total fusion, and self-giving of two enraptured personalities? Seldom. For the covenant of marriage, sympathy, respect, appreciation, benevolence, and trust would suffice. Lifelong companionship should establish integration. It is the state that Thomas [Aquinas] calls "*amicitia*" ("friendship" or "amicable bond"), which probably did not mean an experience of eros smuggled in and legitimated afterward; instead, the word "fondness" (*Neigung*)—so dear to Goethe—which is hardly common today, contains a form of love in its own right, one of the strongest and deepest. C. S. Lewis brilliantly described this in his book *The Four Loves*, including friendship, eros, and agape. This fondness, together with the "one flesh" in the experience of generation, is neither *agape* nor the great passion. But it is enough for many good marriages, even without being extensively developed metaphysically. In the simplest everyday life, such a marriage may have provided support and a framework for countless satisfied couples, for stability and security in fidelity—that are almost unimaginable today—subsumed by the irrevocable solidarity of kinship and the couple's joint responsibility for their offspring. This ethos is based mainly on *pietas*, as Rosenstock-Huessy explains, as a matter of peace between ancestors and grandchildren;[35] it is directed toward responsibility for the past *and* future, toward a sense of duty, a sense of honor, and a tremendous, often unlimited, willingness to sacrifice for the sake of something greater.

28

Kinship-marriage was always *open* to marriage of individuals, and in this, to love-marriage. And oh, how often this may have been successful within

35 Rosenstock-Huessy, *Soziologie*, 2:345.

kinship-marriage. The history of royal marriages, which have always been in the public spotlight, knows of many such "surprises." The love marriage of Louis [IV] with St. Elizabeth of Hungary has become classic—this ice-cold, politically sophisticated connection of small children![36] We hear of the *coup de foudre*, love at first sight, with Emperor Max[imilian I], the last knight, and Mary of Burgundy, with some of the Spanish royal children so unhappily coupled together, and even with the cool rationalist Joseph II of Austria. Nothing prevents the assumption that these events are exemplary for countless people who are not famous.

29

The structure of kinship also corresponds to its most dangerous threat: Infertility, which seems to frustrate its existence, has mostly been attributed to women, and puts continuance in question. This is intensified in dynastic marriages but has played out similarly in lesser situations. Since monogamy blocked the simple way out of having additional wives, succession to the throne, change of rulers on the throne, and civil wars have depended on fertility or infertility. In the private sphere, the tragedy of knowing one is the end of a legacy, to be the last one with which the lineage dies, can be understood today by only a few. This factor

36 Elizabeth of Hungary was betrothed in infancy to the boy who later became King Louis IV; theirs became a loving marriage. Görres writes about the marriage of Louis IV and St. Elizabeth of Hungary in "The Nature of Sanctity," 136–38.

of uncertainty must have cast a horrible shadow on many women's lives, all the more so because in the West, actually incomprehensibly, the very simple East Asian way out, widespread adoption, never prevailed. (Probably, there is a different view of bloodlines there.)

30

Erotic love finds three powerful restraints in kinship-marriage. These restraints depend specifically on the unilinear orientation of kinship-marriage. As an undertaking, generation *should* be the fruit of love. The embrace of the bodies *should* be the height of tenderness, the fusing power of eros that urges this man to become "one flesh" with this woman. But if eros is missing, generation *can* still be accomplished without it. Animals show this possibility at the lowest level. Humans, like animals, can do this, too. But if they choose to do this as morally conscious humans or they are forced to do so, they easily get into serious conflicts. For many, it will be natural and normal. But not for all. Uninhibited selfish sexuality is the very definition of fornication. But even an embrace that is animated by the will to carry out a duty, even driven by the inclination to satisfy the other, is a rather imperfect realization of what might actually be. Such a process is only possible if the mechanism of physical drive is stimulated directly and consciously for this purpose. This cannot seem to a person of refined sensitivity anything other than repulsive. He has to apologize to himself to do this over and over again. He cannot refrain from doing it in lineage-marriage because he was married primarily to do so. What a dilemma! Many married couples will have performed the process as an embarrassing but inevitable action and experienced that "every animal is sad after intercourse"—*omne animal post coitum triste*,[37] not just for animal reasons, but out of their unfulfilled, starving, aggrieved humanness. The fact that the human mind was forced to seek theological, moral justifications—*excusationes*—for sexual intercourse arose presumably much less from the theory of learned texts than from the practice of this certainly extremely frequent experience that simply left behind an innermost feeling of dissatisfaction, a blemish on one's conscience, perhaps a sense of guilt. Hence, one sees the devaluation of sex, which burdens older moral theology—and which, in this context, does not appear to be without reason. Hence, their theory in this area always deals with the two basic terms, "duty" and "pleasure." This is very shocking for their more thin-skinned posterity, but it was "modern" and realistic in the given situation.

31

The second defect is more serious: despite officially very strict marriage laws, there was widespread tacit or open tolerance of adultery as compensation for a union without eros. Here, one thinks of the *maitresse en titre* (chief mistress) in "Christian royal households."

37 Peter McDonald, *The Oxford Dictionary of Medical Quotations*, 118.

32

Third and perhaps worst of all: Within this framework, *eros* is *fundamentally adrift*—and thus becomes the most dangerous power. Many have long written endlessly about the Christian defamation and demonization of eros. In complex charts, the origin of this is traced back to Jansenists, Puritans, Neoplatonists, Manicheans, and so forth. This is from the well-known basic idea that humans have always waited for what professors come up with at their desks in order to behave obediently afterward and to react accordingly. Just have a look at life itself.

Lineage-marriage, we said, must be based on planning. If it is to be realized, engagements must be made as early as possible before eros moves independently and very likely interferes. Eros should occur, if at all, only within marriage. Marriage, however, is not so favorable a soil for eros as it is for fondness—because the essence of eros includes initial distance and uncertainty, the lure of the foreign, the element of surprise, the tension of a vigorous or shy approach, longing, desire, and hesitant resistance. It includes the typical symbolic references of hunting, hunter, arrow, and trap, as well as fortress and conquest. The elements of play, dream, adventure, cunning, and daring make a typical attraction out of the experience, and so eros animates the merely physical processes and boosts it from merely instinctual satiation to the language of personal delight. A clan-marriage between those engaged early offered little space for all of this. That means, and here is the crux: Eros as an *experience* is almost only possible *outside* [of marriage] and even then, as a negative harbinger—as seduction and allowing oneself to be seduced, or as an irresistible harmful incursion into the marriage enclosure. Forbidden things can only be lived out clandestinely. Eroticism generates a whole web of lies, broken promises, hypocrisy, and deception of the other person, as well as the most solemn authorities, in the form of disobedience, rebellion, and multiple harms. This is understandable because experiences of eros are almost only possible in constellations of guilt, such that eros itself generates the stamp of evil and everything that leads to it, which it bestows under the aura of that which is dark, suspect, and dangerous.

33

In this respect, Nietzsche was right in saying that Christianity poisoned the eros it could not eradicate. Sigrid Undset describes these conditions with unmatched authenticity in her tremendous novels set in the Middle Ages in Scandinavia.[38] It is strange how, in spite or because of this, the fairy tales of that era dream of pure love, which prevails against violence and magic, radically demolishing all class barriers: the king's son marries Cinderella; Foundling-Bird marries the girl with no name and thus no lineage; the king's daughter marries the farm boy who is a total stranger,

38 Sigrid Undset, *Kristin Lavransdatter,* and Sigrid Undset, *The Master of Hestviken.*

the youngest son, the son with no inheritance;[39] and so forth.

34

Today, *partner-marriage* faces no opposition in "white cultures," and it is pressing its way into the rest of the world faster and faster. It initially develops as a refinement and humanization of kinship-marriage, not as its contradiction. What is new is the free, spontaneous choice by partners, increasingly also by women; and above all, it is also the place of eros, the rightful place, and it is mainly in this that the happiness of personal love is to be fulfilled. Other than this, it mostly retains the content and values of kinship-marriage. Bearing descendants is still its core; its suitability for this largely determines the choice [of partner] and the erotic taste; having many children is still considered a source of pride and wealth; childlessness is no longer a shame or misfortune but a matter of suffering and an ordeal. In place of extended kinship, what becomes essential is "the household," the home, and the passing on of the tradition of immaterial and material legacy to the descendants. Partner-marriage also serves the future through continuance; it wants to live on in the children—not only to reproduce, but also to produce something better: "My children should be better off."

39 Görres is referring to the three classic fairytales "Cinderella," "Foundling-Bird," and "The Golden Bird."

35

Partner-marriage has expressly vindicated the value and dignity of marriages that have remained *infertile* despite the desire to have children, and has born witness to this many times. Perhaps this has the secret mission of presenting the second side of marriage—perfect companionship, a purely personal relationship—so that marriage is not misunderstood as just an institution for breeding. Such a marriage is its own fruit. Adalbert Stifter, who faced this problem himself, expresses this insight very nicely in the story "Der Waldgänger" ("The Wanderer in the Forest").

36

This development goes surprisingly far back, long before the sociological and economic decline of kinship and long before the emancipation of the individual. Already, Ivo of Chartres, a contemporary of Abelard, insists that a clan's marriage promises do not bind boys in their conscience; instead, only the boys' own yes is binding, even if it differs from the will of the parents. Of course, parental authority in matrimonial matters has lasted an astonishingly long time, right into our day in some countries and circles, in which connections are not recommended but rather "arranged." Oh, the bitterness with which Simone de Beauvoir and other

French feminists talk about this![40] We should remember the novels by Fontane and Stifter. Marriage planning is, above all, the purview of women in the family, a true matriarchy. Still today, pastoral ministers to foreign workers tell us the *nonna*, the grandmother, has the final say among the southern Italians. "For a father's blessing strengthens the houses of the children, but a mother's curse uproots their foundations."[41] Was that deep fear that lasted until well into the nineteenth century, which made many prefer to forgo throughout their lives a marriage that was rejected by parents, really due just to awareness of the Old Testament?

37

Nevertheless, it is a *fable convenue* (a common fable) *simply to conflate partner-marriage and love-marriage.* Unfortunately, today, it is particularly theologians who support this view. According to this, every average and normal marriage is supposed to be the deepest soul-and-body-fusion of two mature people who consciously "totally give and accept"[42] each other in every embrace, and where this is not the case, it would simply not be a marriage or be a marriage that has ended or never came

40 Görres wrote a sharply critical review of Simone de Beauvoir's book *The Second Sex* (Ida Friederike Görres, "'Satanic,' 'An atheistic doctrine of woman': A Review of Simone de Beauvoir's *The Second Sex* [1951].")

41 Sirach 3:9.

42 According to Hotz, "Love is total surrender. In this way, love is the only consummation that can, without compromise, uphold the claim to realize the full humanness (*Menschlichkeit*) of the other person." Hotz, "Wiederverheiratung Geschiedener in der Kirche?" 214.

to be. This view is incomprehensible gibberish in the age of psychology and psychosomatics. This view can only be excused with the assumption that here, too, a kind of collective guilty conscience of celibate men seeks relief by "making amends," that is, to compensate for the long-standing traditional degradation of the "flesh" by theology with a countervailing exuberance. In this way, as in other matters, the child is easily thrown out with the bathwater.

38

Partner-marriages are quite often accommodation-marriages, obligation-marriages, decidely convenience-marriages. Widowers must provide a mother for their toddlers, women a father to their adolescent sons; girls marry out of gratitude; young men marry the brides or widows of fallen friends; old men marry the nurse or housekeeper. Up to the middle of the last century, in the Moravian Church and other strict Protestant groups, brides for departing missionaries were determined by lot or by a decision of the elders—actually, a purely spiritual kinship-marriage.

Alongside the more delicate form of provision-marriage, there is also a rough form: marrying for money and name, the "good catch," marrying into a family, the simple fear of being left single, or marrying because a child is on the way. Of course, these are not ideal motives, but wherever the will to a covenant is honest, these motives are capable of deepening and developing (though, perhaps, this is the least so in actually marrying for money). Therefore, one should not mislead those in these marriages by intensifying the "spirit-aspect" of one's own marriage in a way that at the next hot erotic encounter such people end up denying their marriages, seeing them as none at all by comparison. As far as the heart is concerned, they are just marriages *oriented to hope* like the old kinship-marriages: hope for "real" love, at least for harmony, peace, contentment. The partners may not be able to say, "I love you,"—but they can say, "I will be good to you."

39

The advertisements in the marriage market are very revealing. There is a strikingly strong explicit demand for what the old moral theology called *bonum fidei*: common life, companionship, home, family life, security. There is a remarkably strong emphasis on camaraderie for leisure, as if the majority of life consisted of sport, travel, making music, and so forth. But there is often a veiled offer of one's own youth—still youth!—among the numerous older people who post advertisements. Any talk of children is shockingly rare—as good as never—and if, then of the "baby."[43] One can quite clearly feel the fear of being alone, the weariness of life without attachments, and the fear of aging alone.

43 Görres uses the English word *baby* here.

40

Never directly addressed, but clearly discernible in the range of "erotically valuable" advantages (figure, hair, etc.) and discreetly indicated in the description of the "spirited, vital, tolerant, and so forth" partner, is the fourth property of marriage, called the *remedium concupiscentiae*, that is, the satiation of erotic-sexual desire. Why is that so shocking to modern people who, in a manner never seen before, do not shy away from boldness and directness regarding sex? People cover their ears and make a prudish expression (Luther's [description of marriage as] a "hospital for incurables" is notably coarser).[44] They distance themselves, when they are theologians, embarrassed by the ancients, or they try to attribute deep metaphysical speculations to the word sex or impose such speculations on it. Sure, these interpretations are very beautiful and edifying. But to start with, is this matter not actually much simpler? Is the desire for an "orderly sex life" indecent in itself? The desire for a way out of the jungle of hardships and embarrassments that an unordered, unsatisfied sexuality represents in practical terms? It has always been there, this misery, in various forms, for the unsettled bachelor—be it, as someone put it drastically, "commuting between brothel and confessional," or the more appealing long-term relationship, "also something for the mind," but burdened from the start with the planned farewell for the purpose of a

44 Martin Luther, "A Sermon on the Estate of Marriage," 632.

better marriage, with the fear of the illegitimate child, perhaps tragedy, blackmail, suicide; or the even more strained relationship with married women. For many young women, there is the relationship "out of pity," out of vanity, or as a tactic for getting married, which then was of no use. These "old-fashioned" figures of fate have given way to promiscuity as a matter of course—whether one regards it as a minor evil or as a further descent, at least not a solution. Paul's statement that to prevent fornication, every man should have a wife and every woman a husband—already a Jewish rule[45]—is probably somehow the basis of the term *remedium*. If one is not exempted due to a vocation or a condition, one has to deal with the matter somehow, and if this desire to "get it in order" is one part of the will to marry, it is certainly not shameful.

41

But if the *remedium concupiscentiae* moves from the edge to the center, the disintegration of the marriage has already begun. The white race has already positioned itself within this far-reaching, fateful trend. There is nothing on which the human community is inherently dependent in so many ways as it is on the marital relationship. A wise old minister once said to me: "Good spouses not only make each other father and mother, they are also father and mother, brother and sister, friends and companions, yes, each is even the

45 See 1 Corinthians 7:9.

other's child—it is the whole rainbow of love." This is also part of the meaning of childless marriage.

In sex-marriage, this whole rainbow is erased; the interaction is narrowed down to pure lust for the body. People who find a convenience-marriage immoral in terms of the human creature and the formation of the person see no problem in a convenience-marriage for the greatest possible pleasure.

A different genre of writing, one that Catholic marriage counselors unfortunately also take part in, educates about this and includes porn films. Exotic harem practices and brothel tricks are supposed to fill the emptiness that the retreat from parenthood leaves. "Instead of children, they have problems," mocked Spengler;[46] now, they are just being replaced by group sex and partner swapping. Do not be persuaded that human *tenderness*—an eminently *emotional* behavior!—needs that training. Of course, unnecessary inhibitions of shyness, awkwardness, and false fears of conscience should be resolved gently and prudently so that the body learns its love language—but precisely its own personal, individual language, not the mimicking of film poses. The author of *The Naked Ape* is not even right in recommending that to bond, the couple should "make the shared [sexual] activities of the pair more complicated and more rewarding."[47] Experienced

46 Görres is paraphrasing Oswald Spengler: "Instead of children they have emotional conflicts." Oswald Spengler, *Der Untergang des Abendlandes*, 2:124.

47 Desmond Morris, *The Naked Ape*, 65. In the German edition of Morris's book, the word "activities" is translated as *Sexualhandlungen* (sexual activities). Morris, *Der nackte Affe*, 60.

doctors know that this kind of business inevitably leads to weariness, disgust, and a raging desire for variety. Such a relationship stands still far below the animal-“marriage” that serves for reproduction, even if anthropologists have recently begun to encourage us by assuring: “Baboons also occasionally perform sexual gestures without connection to reproduction.” How comforting, how affirming for humans at last to find a valid role model!

42

What binds marriage “forever”?

The “small” infatuation, erotic attraction, is known to be the most volatile thing there is. Its symbol is Cupid, son of Venus, not Eros, the great demon. Cupid—*Cupido*—the toddler: curious, fickle, frivolous! With his wings, he “flits” like a butterfly from stimulus to stimulus, from satiety to weariness. He succumbs to the extinguishing of the “attractions.” Psychologically speaking, he lives from projections, desired images, placed on the partner like a costume. But projections wander like St. Elmo’s fire, sometimes settling on one, now on the other, and Cupid follows their flickering like a wandering checkered-skipper butterfly.

43

It is different with the *passion* of love, the great eros. It can ignite at the dawn of an encounter, anticipatory recognition of a *you* who will be ascertained, the dawning light of a sun for life. Baader calls it "divine phantasmagoria"[48]—exaggerating and transfiguring at the beginning, nevertheless real and corrected by the course of life, but confirmed, authentic fruit of an authentic blossom; it is for many the great destiny of a couple encountering each other, the genius of being able to feel. "Better agony with you than happiness with another!" Abelard and Heloise are examples of ill-fated love. "Better to be called a whore than to be the queen of the Western world!" she writes to him after years of imposed separation.[49] (Imposed by him!) Sigrid Undset's epic novel *Kristin Lavransdatter* has a classic description of such an inseparable marriage of misfortune.

Great passion believes the question of time and duration is removed. "For love is strong as death, jealousy is cruel as the grave. . . . Many waters cannot quench love, neither can floods drown it."[50] And *The Poetic Edda* responds to the Hebrew *Song of Songs* from the remote region of the Thule:

Ever with grief
    and all too long

48 Franz Xaver von Baader, "Sätzte aus der erotischen Philosophie," paragraph 18.

49 Perhaps here Görres is paraphrasing one of these passages: "Noble queen, more adorned with her own voluntary dishonor than with a royal wreath!" or: "When she is a queen of one devoted heart, then she has a kingdom that sufficeth for her ambition." Orlando Williams Wight, Peter Abelard, Héloïse, Alphonse de Lamartine, *Lives and Letters of Abelard and Heloise*, 230, 13, respectively.

50 Song of Songs 8:6–7.

Are men and women
born in the world;
But yet we shall live
our lives together,
Sigurth and I . . .[51]

Yet, unfortunately, we know from poetry, history, biographies, autobiographies, and everyday experience that even such love can die, though it does not have to. This is why the greatest tragedy often stands alongside the bliss of love. "Love that died never was love" is a youthful dream or a very clever alibi. Even beautiful, ardently spirited human love, which seems to merge couples irrevocably, is dissolved again when eros appears in an altered form, a form of greater mesmerization on the horizon. Consider Goethe and Charlotte von Stein. It is not without reason that the poets speak of lightning, assault, a tidal wave, fever, intoxication, and madness; they speak of eros as the flooding, violent element, stronger than the person who becomes its prey.

44

We do not want it to be true, and yet it happens again and again. Why do we consider this such a surprise? Love is subject to death because we are subject to death. It is a part, even the most beautiful part, of our

51 Anonymous, "Helreith Brynhildar," 446. The title of this poem, "Helreith Brynhildar," may be translated as "Brynhild's Hell-Ride." *The Poetic Edda* is a collection of Old Norse narrative poems.

mortal, fallen nature, our "flesh," which also includes the psyche. The memory of all humankind preserves the never-ending complaint that all beauty withers, all fires burn out, that love dies like the body that it transfigures and holds spellbound.

45

The Greek myth that Aphrodite appears as the daughter of the sea, of this deep, phantasmic primal force, as change and inconsistency itself, and that she is connected to the god of fire, as well as the god of war, strife, and hatred, should really make us think twice.

In any case, everyone agrees that great passion is the exception and not the norm, that people experience it as a temporary experience and do not choose it themselves.

It would be completely nonsensical to demand it as the basis of the consensus for entry into marriage, or to let the duration of the covenant depend on it.

46

Next to eros, there is "fondness," as already mentioned: unromantic, sober, eminently capable of development, very mundane, and psychologically uninteresting. But with kindness, humor, and patience, it is what is adequate for an innumerable number of marriages; it is a tough clay that can mature into the most beautiful "benevolent love," even without *amor complacentiae* (love arising from attraction) and *amor concupiscentiae* (love arising from desire), the erotic components. From Goethe, of all people, who knew all the ecstasies and abysses of the great passions, comes the statement:

> It [fondness] is what actually makes a person happy if he knows how to retain it. It is worth considering for yourself that habit can take the place of passionate love.... [I]t does not require a comely presence rather a comfortable one, but then it is invincible. It takes a lot to give up a relationship that has become habitual. It exists against everything that is in opposition: dissatisfaction, resentment, anger are nothing against what is familiar; yes, it outlasts contempt, hatred. I do not know whether a novelist has ever succeeded in fully portraying the likes of this.[52]

This is a strange observation, the ambivalence of which should not be overlooked.

Fondness can warm up into love; passion can cool down to mere tolerance. The relationship can spread from outside to inside—

52 Johann Wolfgang von Goethe, *Berliner Ausgabe. Kunsttheoretische Schriften und Übersetzungen*, 18:529–30. Regarding Goethe's remark, "I do not know whether a novelist has ever succeeded in fully portraying the likes of this," I would like to suggest that the novelist Ann Howard Creel succeeds, at least in part, in depicting a marriage in which "fondness" outlasts "contempt" in her novel *The Magic of Ordinary Days* (also released as a film directed by Brent Shields); in time and due to the couple's fidelity, as Görres describes in this volume, "love is not its root, rather its fruit." Translator.

This your beauty made,
brought me to love,
with great desire.[53]

—but, also, aging, illness, even ugliness can awaken a new, deep tenderness. In dispassionately spending time together, one can unexpectedly discover the body of the other as something unanticipatedly precious. This fluctuation has no rules.

47

It goes without saying, and has been tried and tested countless times, that *children* can bind a couple most intimately, be it as the most delightful gift that lovers give each other, *the* fulfillment of wishes, or as a new part of life that those more focused on achievement and other work come to understand gradually. How gratitude binds! The thousands of small experiences of joy and worry form a reliable cement. But failing to see the ambivalence here would be romanticization or sentimentality. Imposed children are the most terrible burden; the mother's hatred teaches us about this phenomenon that is not terribly rare; those who glorify motherly love keep silent about this. Raising children can cause serious conflicts between parents. Also, the shared yoke, the constriction of coexistence, especially in today's apartments, can create that constant irritation and claustrophobia that incite outbursts and fluctuate

53 From the German folk song "Ade zur guten Nacht" ("Farewell to a Good Night"). Anonymous, "Ade zur guten Nacht," 61.

explosively. Here, in the case of marriages entered into "soberly," the unconscious flammable matter can accumulate until the slightest erotic attraction from outside becomes a match on a powder keg. In fact, such marriages require vigilance that is equivalent to that needed for celibacy, unless tenderness and warmth have developed, at least out of habit.

48

What binds forever? Covenant, law, and grace—that is, sacrament.

All these three are not outside or ancillary to love, nor are they a substitute for it. Rather they are the ground, the enclosure, in which the modes of love I have mentioned find the complement of their natural shortcomings; they find their integration into each other, interior and external support, the dynamism of growth toward maturity. Also, last but not least, and as the most important element, these three are the *healing power* in the event of impending decay as when a tear occurs, the *healing power* which, unseen, is part of the deepest mystery of the *resurrection* of the dead—literally so.

49

Mature couples and young couples are like bundles of wheat and grapes at mealtime.[54] As a Finnish saying has it: “God provides the field, but not the plow. God provides the well, but not the jug.” A covenant involves order, namely desired order, not the unconsciousness of an insect colony. A covenant does not grow out of itself. A covenant is given and entered into. It is not something one finds; it does not just “happen,” it *should* happen. A covenant is an action and an achievement. A covenant has a certain form and is something distinct.

50

A covenant binds. First, in *word*. A person has needs. In the “sober” motivations for marriage, a person may not, by a long shot, “give himself away totally and with abandonment.” But he can give and keep his word. The new wedding rite [of 1969] has become almost alarmingly reserved and economical. Each person merely promises to “be faithful,” and the “*yes*, to love and to respect” sounds like something haltingly added-on, like a possibility that one concedes. If they then exchange rings as a “sign of loyalty and love,” this “love” does not necessarily mean more than resolute readiness for ever-increasing devotion. But this much is something anyone can promise.

54 Görres is alluding to the way wheat and grapes form basic components of a meal as well as the components of the sacrament of the Eucharist.

The weight of "giving one's word" has waned dreadfully; it has become as light as paper. In its "fidelity and faith," it once weighed so heavily that the problem could legitimately arise as to whether the engagement was not an irrevocable first step in marriage, and dissolution of an engagement brought shame to both families. In political and social life, fidelity to oaths and vows outweighed any other duty of conscience. I know that such seriousness is now slandered as feudalistic utilitarian ethics. But it is the highest testimony to the spirit-nature of the human being and the early, pre-reflexive recognition of this nature: one's word "concentrates" the will, puts it into the world objectively as a matter of concern. "What differentiates humans from animals is that they can make a promise and keep it" (Nietzsche).[55] Actually, an era that idolizes planning like ours should be open to the fact that humans can exercise self-control preemptively. To make matters worse, role models are missing all around. Political oaths have led ties of loyalty to the point of becoming an absurd farce. In her concept of marriage and religious vows, the Church alone protects knowledge of this human sovereignty amid all the determinisms of the environment.

55 Görres may be paraphrasing this passage by Nietzsche: "The breeding of an animal that can *promise*—is not this just that very paradox of a task which nature has set itself in regard to man? Is it not this the very problem of man?" Friedrich Nietzsche, *On the Genealogy of Morals*, 61.

51

The marriage covenant binds secondly through *bodily* surrender, the "consummation" of the marriage. This is the simplest and most obvious sense of "becoming one flesh." It is sad and confusing that today, two reductionist interpretations blur the straightforward power of this type of consummation. There is either the "spirit-izing" exaggeration, which unfortunately can also be found in the new wedding rite [of 1969]: "That they *no longer* form *two*, but rather *one body, one heart and one soul.*"[56] Does the Lord not say explicitly: they will be *two* in one *flesh*[57]—"flesh" in the sense of the Old Covenant, which is more than "body"—as the whole structure of life, within which precisely the two *remain*, with all the ways they are different, as well as the tension and to have to accomplish and deepen the union ever anew? The other mitigation is that the physical union is a mere sex process—indifferent, performable innumerable times with any partner. Since the concept of *virginity* has almost been eliminated, the great poignancy, that is, the pathos, the seriousness of the first surrender, its symbolic value for the whole, has become almost indecipherable. "How," even theologians ask, "can one night, the first night, existentially

56 It is unclear which text Görres is quoting. Perhaps she is referring to the following section of the Novus Ordo Catholic Nuptial Blessing. In the official English translation, it is "that they might no longer be two, but one flesh." International Commission on English in the Liturgy Corporation (ICEL), *The Order of Celebrating Matrimony*, 2013.

57 See Genesis 2:24, Matthew 19:5, Mark 10:8, and Ephesians 5:31.

consummate a marriage? Does it not require many years?" Consummated marriage does not mean that it is either perfect or that it has withstood the test. It is a beginning, but it is irreversible. It is *the birth of the couple* out of man and woman *into a "procreator,"* an image of the Creator in Creation, which happens only through the bodies, even when, through no fault of their own, this beginning cannot be fully realized in fertility.

For this reason alone, physical intercourse should not yet be part of the period of engagement. It is a handing over and bonding through vitality and organs of propagation for propagation. It could already be sealed by a child. This could, of course, lead to the question of whether the deliberately truncated act that excludes generation—such as through the pill and choice of timing!—is really "consummation" in this sense? In the case of authentic marriage, would not consummation be regarded as a symbolic indication of readiness? When generation is a cosmic as well as a Christian function, the (real) first consummation is the initiation. "I think the time is near," wrote Hans Asmussen, "where it is also medically proven that the physical fellowship of the spouses also changes the biological structure of the spouses. This is all just the outer expression for the inner change, which, unfortunately, so few spouses pay attention to."[58] Ancient peoples seem to have known more about the fact that, in a very precise sense, the bodily fellowship creates "one flesh," a type of "blood

58 Hans Asmussen, *Das Geheimnis der Liebe*, 48. Ida Görres wrote a review of this book in 1963: Ida Friederike Görres, "Neues über die Liebe? Asmussen, Hans *Das Geheimnis der Liebe*," 237–38.

relationship" in addition to the relationship through lineage. The marriage laws and the new barriers to incest established by them seem to indicate this.

Like every birth, this beginning initiates a process of becoming. A marriage that is becoming—that has just become a marriage—is a marriage like the way an embryo is a human. The marriage's undeveloped state gives it as little justification for its destruction as the child's undeveloped state would be justification for abortion. For this commencement can grow into the miracle of the marital union that coalesces everything together: sexuality and friendship, eroticism and sacrifice, the urge to reproduce and the highest human longing for fulfillment in another, passion, play, trust, awe, everything that the ancients ascribed to very different, often quite hostile, deities. This seal of unity is a sign of the One God.

52

We need the *law* in order to keep the covenant. Of its own accord, the covenant is concerned with legality and law because marriage also has its indispensable public side. "Marriage law," says Ratzinger, "is not an external ingredient of self-sufficient love; it is part of the nature of human marriage because man is inherently a law-oriented being."[59] People cannot perpetually live out rights, even recognized rights, without law. Every honest person knows how prone the often-invoked

59 Ratzinger, "Zur Theologie der Ehe," 586.

mature conscience is to corruption as soon as it faces a rush of strong passions, how it is able and willing to engage in every bit of twisting, every bit of sophistry, every self-suggestion. All abuse of office, which has, in fact, been carried out and will repeat itself, all human sacrifices not answered for in front of an often-inhumane jurisprudence, do not negate these simple facts. The wisest, that is, the most independent, the most original, the most fearless, have confirmed this basic truth: "It is better for you to be wronged than for the world to be without law . . . It is better for injustices to occur than for them to be remedied in an unjust manner"[60] (Goethe).

Even Karl Marx says with unmistakable clarity, "Nobody is forced to contract a marriage, but everyone, once they decide to marry, must be *forced* to choose to obey the laws of marriage. Whoever marries does not invent the laws of marriage any more than a swimmer creates nature, inventing the laws of water and gravity. Marriage can, therefore, not submit to one's caprice, but his caprice must submit to marriage."[61]

53

Our contemporaries have a hard time with law. We already discussed at the outset the general allergy to authority and permanence. Both of these qualities are part of law. Deep within the Church, it has become

60 Johann Wolfgang von Goethe, *Goethes Sprüche in Prosa*, 109.

61 Karl Marx, "The Divorce Bill," 1:307.

fashionable among theologians to treat the law from the get-go as a bogeyman, as something repressive and despotic, as an insult against the maturity of adult Christians and an attack on their "freedom." Law, a Jewish intrusion against the Gospel, is to be viewed with a suspicion that is ready-to-pounce, with really "Protestant"—and in no way "Gospel-oriented"—fear and arrogance pushing back against legalism. As if this always had to be negative: infantile, servile, immature, a forbidden clinging to imaginary security. This distorted image exists, often as a compulsive neurotic disposition, as a product of misguided upbringing, but it is neither a norm nor a must. We must free ourselves from this strategic suggestion and learn to look at the archetype. Here, we can—without getting flustered—learn something from the Jews to whose piety in the Old Testament we are still verbally deferential: their *love* for the law as the expression of the Will of God, their gratitude for the law as a directive, a path, a staff, a light, nourishment—the way the Psalms, especially Psalm 118[/119],[62] ceaselessly praise the law. Can we even imagine a "Festival of Joy for the Torah" [Simchat Torah], joy for the divine gift of guidance?

"Where obedience is rooted, Love as well is very near," says the ballad of Bayadere [by Goethe].[63] The

62 This psalm opens with, "Blessed are those whose way is blameless, who walk in the law of the LORD!" (118/119:1). Görres's identification of this as Psalm 118 indicates she was using the Vulgate numbering. In later translations, such as the RSVCE, this would be Psalm 119.

63 Johann Wolfgang von Goethe, "The God and the Bayadere," 49.

reverse might be even more true: "If love is in one's spirit, obedience will not be far off."

We encounter God's Will so rarely, so seldom nakedly and directly as His Truth. In both instances, a medium—the commandment as well as Revelation—is required. Only dealing with both and doing so with faithfulness, humility, and gratitude trains us to recognize them "out-of-context"—in conscience, "voiced," and not to be confused with the hallucinations of desire and imagination. What is faith in one is obedience in the other. Both are manifestations of *trust*; both are a risk, but undertaken confidently.

54

The law is full of mysteries, as is faith. Anyone from the outside can toss a wet blanket on how we view each of these two, but each of these can only gradually be understood from the inside and in the process of carrying it out. In fact, God hides His Will in the law the way He hides His Light in dogma: both are "in a [protective] nutshell." In both instances, the shell is hard, and it pushes back—and one must not stop at the outer shell. Obedience and faith are forms of worship.

55

Gustave Thibon, the philosopher and friend of Simone Weil, says that in eras when customs decay, obedience to the commandment becomes an expression of love and freedom.

56

The third [thing that binds marriage, after covenant and law] is *grace*. It is the sacrament, the inexplicable, the ineffable, that which defies definition, the most secret transformation and fulfillment of marriage, which is already naturally so "wonder-full," through Revelation and faith.

57

Theologians and exegetes today assure us with peculiar emphasis that "the New Testament has no doctrine of marriage."[64] The individual arguments, I must say, do not convince me at all. They often seem extremely artificial, flat, and sketchy to me. But that is not at issue here. Let them have their arguments (*habeant*). Of course, the New Testament has no more a marriage doctrine than it does a christology, a doctrine of sacraments, a doctrine of the Trinity. But this just confirms the ancient Catholic article of faith: that Scripture alone is *not* sufficient and absolutely requires further explanation and interpretation by the Church—that, yes, this is expressly the work of the Holy Spirit promised by the Lord in the Church: "he will teach you all things, and bring to your remembrance all that I have said to you."[65]

64 Hotz, for example, writes, "In the NT [New Testament] there is no doctrine of marriage." Hotz, "Wiederverheiratung Geschiedener in der Kirche?," 214.

65 John 14:26.

58

But let us also reflect entirely matter-of-factly: Is this "lack" central? Over long periods of time how little did the faithful read the Scriptures; how much was theology a secret doctrine, as unfamiliar to most believers as higher mathematics and physics are to us. In spite of this, the influence of faith has been tremendous and has changed the face of the world, including in matters of marriage. The words of Jesus and the Apostles are seed-words, words for fermentation—who would have demanded a systematic treatise from them?—embedded into the marriage traditions and customs of populations, Jewish law, Roman law, Greek philosophy, tribal customs of barbarians; they slowly, unnoticed, transformed these three measures of flour [covenant, law, grace] into the bread we live on. It is not only historical, sociological, economic circumstances that have gradually overcome the old sex-marriage. It has also crumbled from the inside—not just like an old house from which life moves out, but like the protective leaves of a bud for new life. "All beginnings are invisible."

59

"All the great powers of history were first formed in the secrecy of the heart" (Hugo Rahner).[66]

66 Görres may be paraphrasing a passage from Hugo Rahner, *Symbole der Kirche*, 41.

60

Marriage that is monogamous and happens only once, I already said, is interconnected with the One and Only God. The human should love Him, cling to Him, "with all your heart, and with all your soul, and with all your mind."[67] Christian marriage is, among other things, an attempt to "translate" this "model" into the exclusive covenant between two people. A new relationship with God and a new understanding of God created a new understanding of the self and also transformed the relationships between people. Holy matrimony grew as a living fruit on the tree of humanity (*Menschtum*) transformed by the Church, not out of paragraphs and treatises. Not only did a new law come into the world, but a new *soul* emerged. The text from Gertrud von le Fort's *Hymns to the Church* still applies:

> I have fashioned you for a thousand years and longer, I blessed all your fathers and mothers with the cross . . .
>
> You have grown subtle, soul, you have become like a silky flax that it has taken long to spin.[68]

The life and spirit of the faithful are concrete experiences, historical facts, which crystallized in institutions and, in turn, enriched the interpretation of the Word, were re-illuminated by the deepened interpretation,

67 Matthew 22:37.

68 Gertrud von le Fort, *Hymns to the Church*, 111.

and so forth. It is an unbreakable cycle, never to be fully analyzed retrospectively, at most manifested at watershed moments.

61

What is new is expressed, for example, in the psychologically and sociologically inexplicable resistance that the men of the Church, themselves brought up in the old tribal ethos and imbued with it, put up against the wish for divorce in the infertility dramas of dynasties, even though Roman and Germanic law permitted divorce and remarriage. Even when infertility threatened to ruin the kinship-lineage (*gens*), which the bishops and popes still understood as the highest worldly value and an ethical duty, or when, as happened all too often, changing political constellations destroyed the "alliance character" of a royal-marriage and better connections were offered, the Church has always fought for the rejected women, not only in the case of Henry VIII in the strife over England.

When it comes to the lower classes, similar things are repeated, tentatively in the beginning, then growing, first in marginal social situations of people outside the clan and its rights. Merovingian bishops, for example, insist on the validity of slave-marriage against the seizure by their masters, who want to separate and conjoin them with others—quite legal in a juridical sphere in which the slave is not a person. It is similar with other outsiders, refugees, emigrants, also sons and daughters who defend a personal bond against the clan's marriage plan. For Pope Nicholas I, is it really *only* adoption of Roman law—"the consensus creates marriage"—which creates this breakthrough of the rock-solid customary law of kinship? If only one of the two refuses to consent, then no marriage has been achieved, despite the order of the highest competent authority, whether father, clan chief, or prince, despite the wedding celebration and even completion of the consummation taking place. But centuries ago, are not the martyrologies, the legends of the saints, full of stories of virgins who refuse kinship- and status-marriage to the point of martyrdom because they are engaged to Christ? An expression of unprecedented freedom—female freedom!—long before the "birth of the individual."

62

At first, this new experience seems to be directed *against* marriage. Alexius leaves his bride on the wedding night;[69] the brothers of Bernard of Clairvaux separate from their wives. Nevertheless—nothing can be proven here, of course—it is precisely this constant example of the absolute love of God that has also inspired the love of spouses and opened up a tremendous new possibility, and this at times when a wife was actually a man's "most precious possession." Conversely, the monk takes from "earthly" love all the basic images of "bridal" mystique that erotic

69 Alexius left his bride the night of their wedding, without consecrating the marriage, for a celibate life of seeking God. Görres wrote a short story inspired by his life: Ida Friederike Görres, "The Bride of Alexius."

vocabulary has to offer him. Here, too, the reciprocity is immeasurable.

63

In light of this, the faithful today encounter a tough and painful *indignation* in the practice of the hierarchy, which grants all honor and a Church wedding not only to guilty priests, who, to the great indignation of the congregation, lived for longer or shorter periods with a concubine and left their [priestly] office for the sake of a woman, but the hierarchy grants this even to monks with solemn vows, after many years of profession. The fact that monastery life can be unbearable for people for justifiable reasons is just as understandable as it is in married life for married people. We do not understand, however, that total divorce is being used instead of separation. We have been taught that the sacramentality of the marriage covenant consists explicitly in the fact that it is the one, general sign in the re-execution of the covenant between Christ and the Church; the second sign—exceptional sign—is full consecration to God in an order. Consecration to God once overtook even the marriage bond—one thinks of Nicholas of Flüe.[70]

70 St. Nicholas of Flüe, also known as Brother Klaus (1417–1487), was a Swiss man who experienced a call to become a hermit after he had been married about twenty-five years and he and his wife had ten children. With the consent of his wife, he left to become a hermit.

64

Today, for the sake of a late desire to marry, voluntary and sworn devotion to God is annulled. Then why should the poor layperson persevere? It seems to us, painfully, that through this practice, the Church is sawing vigorously at the branch from which indissoluble marriage grows.

65

Peculiar factors contributed to the humanization of marriage. For example, who would have expected that reflecting on the *marriage of Mary* with Joseph has made an explicit contribution to recognizing the weight of consent, the binding "yes," even if no marital bodily union follows? In the Middle Ages, not just in Roman and Germanic law, the distinctions in this regard between a marriage being contracted and consummated are established, as well as the emphasis on love and friendship that does not depend on sex and erotic fulfillment.

66

The "Evolution of Chastity" (as Teilhard de Chardin called it)[71] through the concrete unfolding of faith in

71 Görres is referring to the 1934 essay "L'Evolution de la Chasteté" ("The Evolution of Chastity") by Teilhard de Chardin. The only footnote in the German edition of *What Binds Marriage Forever* was placed at this point in the book (presumably by Görres rather than after her death by an editor). It

teaching and life should not be underestimated in its scope and breadth, and it should never be excluded from a Christian conversation; rather, this should constantly permeate it. Certainly, the ethics of many pagans have high praise for chastity and condemnation of unchastity, but often nearly restricted just to women. (So, too, it is worth considering why women were effectively considered and treated as the exemplary embodiment of both extremes.) For Jews and pagans of all kinds as well, chastity, in terms of untouchability, is the "honor" of women par excellence. Violation of this is a disgrace; the violent violation is "desecration," which the girl, the woman, can actually evade or atone for by suicide. Consider Lucretia![72] Such an assessment far exceeds the somewhat platitudinous ethical definition that classifies chastity only as a variant of the moderation that must also curb the other animal appetites, more like

---

reads: "Presented in Henri de Lubac's masterful commentary on Teilhard's 'Hymn of the Eternal Female,' Einsiedeln 1968"; that is, Henri de Lubac, *The Eternal Feminine: A Study on the Poem by Teilhard de Chardin*. René Hague, the translator of this book from French to English, translates the title of the essay "L'Evolution de la Chasteté" as "The Evolution of Chastity" (see pages 48–65).

However, in the German edition of this book to which Görres refers—Pierre Teilhard de Chardin, *Hymne an das ewig Weibliche, mit einem Kommentar von Henri de Lubac*—the translator Hans Urs von Balthasar translates "L'Evolution de la Chasteté" as "Entwicklung der Keuschheit" ("Development of Chastity") (63–83). Yet Görres, in spite of the fact she refers the reader to von Balthasar's translation, herself translates the title of the essay "L'Evolution de la Chasteté" into German as "Evolution der Keuschheit" ("Evolution of Chastity").

72 Lucretia was a Roman noblewoman who was raped by the son of a tyrannical king. After obtaining an oath of vengeance from her father and her husband, she committed suicide. An enraged mob drove the tyrannical king out of Rome, which led to the founding of the Roman Republic in 509 B.C.

an aesthetic and pedagogical category, the violations of which appear more as unaesthetic, shameful, and ridiculous than evil.

We even read with surprise as Francis de Sales, who understood much about eros, describes the (legitimate) physical joy of marriage as just an analogy to the joy of eating: one should enjoy it impartially, happily, gratefully, at ease—"but only a lowly person is still thinking about the food after the meal."[73] This may apply to humans, even to a Christian, insofar as one merely represents a well-behaved animal, that is, is at home in the most primitive dimension of his existence.

67

In this regard, the important topics in Josef Pieper's still unsurpassed essay on "Temperance" should be read. Already with Thomas [Aquinas's] consideration of ancient ethics, completely new terms and standards, as well as observations, come to light. For example,

> Chastity realizes in the province of sex the order which corresponds to the truth of the world and of man both as experienced and as revealed, and which accords with the twofold form of this

73 Görres appears to be paraphrasing St. Francis de Sales, who writes: "It is an infallible mark of a wayward, infamous, base, abject, and degraded mind to think about food and drink before mealtime, much more so to delight ourselves later with the pleasure we had in eating, keeping it alive in words and imagination and taking delight in recalling the sensual satisfaction had in swallowing those bits of food" (Part III, Chapter 39). Francis de Sales, *Introduction to the Devout Life*, 228.

truth—not that of unveiled evidence alone, *but that of veiled evidence also—that is, mystery.*[74]

Or:

Unchastity begets a blindness of spirit which practically excludes all understanding of the goods of the spirit; unchastity splits the power of decision; conversely, the virtue of chastity more than any other makes man capable and ready for *contemplation.*[75]

Above all, however, chastity and unchastity are from now on completely immersed in the mystery of the "*becoming human*" in the Incarnation that has forever changed the meaning, value, and weight of the "flesh." When Thomas [Aquinas], for example, says, "Christ is the chief Lord (*principalis Dominus*), the first owner of our bodies, and that one who uses his body in a manner contrary to order, injures Christ the Lord Himself,"[76] that is simply how he interprets the end of the sixth chapter of the First Letter to the Corinthians:

Do you not know that your body is a temple of the Holy Spirit within you, which you have from God? *You are not your own*; you were bought with a price . . . Shun immorality. Every other sin which a man

74 Josef Pieper, "Temperance," in *The Four Cardinal Virtues*, 158. Italics added by Görres.

75 Pieper, "Temperance," 159–60. Italics added by Görres. Cf. Ephesians 5:32.

76 Pieper, "Temperance," 156.

> commits is outside the body; but the immoral man sins against his own body . . . The body is not meant for immorality, but for the Lord, and the Lord for the body . . . So *glorify God in your body*![77]

68

The enviable beautiful old Anglican wedding rite contains the statement by the man: "With my body I thee worship." It can hardly be translated [into German], because "worship" spans the entire spectrum from honor, worship, religious, cultic worship to "adoration." In this, it makes the woman's body the object of religious awe—and this is probably mutual, even if it is not said. Every man's body resembles the figure of Christ, every female body the body that gave birth to God.

Not only are the spouses, like every fellow believer, "the brother for whom Christ died"[78] for each other. And the passage about the millstone around the neck certainly extends within this relationship to "annoying,"[79] seducing, shocking, confusing the one who is younger, defenseless, less secure. Rather, unchastity, in general, and especially within marriage, becomes a sacrilege, an outrage in the sanctuary. And all of this is in addition to what I will not discuss further here because the section would be too long: the "natural"

77 1 Corinthians 6:19–20, 18, 13, 20. Italics added by Görres.

78 1 Corinthians 8:11.

79 See Matthew 18:6, Mark 9:42, and Luke 17:2.

mystery of parenthood as participation in the work of Creation and in the completion of the world that leads to Christ's Second Coming.

69

(From the exaggerated pendulum swing against overemphasis on the Sixth Commandment of days gone by, the fact that today, religious dissemination in all its branches—in school, sermons, literature, and mass media—hardly dares to talk about chastity and unchastity is a calamity of unforeseeable consequences. While the negative, most noxious "education" on the subject of sex showers down in unprecedented abundance and relentlessness on youth in particular and fills the whole environment, positive leadership and formation of conscience remain simply absent. Has a young generation ever been so let down in this regard? With this, cornerstones that are indispensable for every marriage are disappearing.)

70

The medieval, scholastic concept of marriage is shouted down today as barbaric and primitive, or at best antiquated and stoic. Then how is it that it yielded the most delicate and most spiritual interpretations that exceed sky-high beyond the "mere morality" and sociology [of today]?

Bertold of Regensburg: "Marriage is one of the highest among the seven holy things that God has on earth. That is why it should be without falsehood."[80] "It is the most powerful symbol of the most sacred bonds."

In Thomas Aquinas, marriage epitomizes the unity of human and divine nature in Christ, and therefore it perpetuates the Incarnation. *Like the Eucharist*, it is a pledge of future glory. As a sacrament, it is admittedly only a sign, and it will cease, like all signs will cease. But the reality is that it represents, remains, and is fulfilled in the next world because, just as it has its archetype in the love of God, it is also the sign of the coming fellowship of the human with God.

Or there is the utterly astonishing "mystique of the couple" of Cornelius a Lapide in his commentary on Genesis:

> In the creation of Adam and Eve, God wanted to replicate His eternal procreation and breathing of new life. Just as He begets the Son from eternity and breathes into life the Holy Spirit out of the Son, so in time He created Adam in His image, as it were he was created as His son, and from him, He created Eve *so that she would be the love of Adam*, the way the Holy Spirit is facets of the love of God.[81]

Eccentric and elusive? All the same, it attests how deeply internalized and spiritualized the understanding

80 Karl Unkel, *Berthold von Regensburg*, 44. Translated by Bryson.

81 The translation of this passage from Cornelius a Lapide is my translation from the German text in Görres's book into English. (Who translated the German text from the original Latin— perhaps Görres, perhaps someone else—is unknown.) For one translation of this passage from Latin into English, see Cornelius a Lapide, SJ. *Commentary on Genesis 1–3*, 145–46. *Translator.*

was already even in the era of the most far-reaching "marriage commerce."

71

The fifth chapter of Ephesians seems to be of highest importance for the development of the awareness of monogamous, indissoluble marriage. Here, the man is enjoined to love his wife as Christ loves His Church—in the way that He could "sanctify" His flock: namely for its salvation.[82] The man has always wanted to make himself "look impressive" with the beauty, the pomp, the appearance of his wife. For the simplest courtship, the young man buys a scarf, a ribbon, a necklace for the young lady. The woman has always wanted to see her husband "in the lead," wanted to be proud of him; this ambition is probably one of the most decisive factors in economic and social drive. Now, this elementary fondness has been transposed into a new dimension: "without spot or wrinkle."[83] In other words, husband and wife should *sanctify* each other, help each other to the height of their human, spiritual, and Christian potential. And what this is going to cost is told straightaway: everything. The Lord Himself was able to do this only through suffering, the Cross, and death. This itself is what yields the most profound dimension of indissolubility. Working together, for each other, takes an entire lifetime. It is already so merely on the

82 Ephesians 5:26.

83 Ephesians 5:27.

level of nature. How should covenant, love, loyalty, companionship be realized, if not one after the other? Humans are historical beings, and if one "completely" accepts another as "historical," this means: with their past, at present, and for their whole future. Nobody can present themselves, what they "are," all at once. Each person "un-folds," "un-furls," as our [German] language well knows.[84] How long it takes until a person "comes into his own," finds himself! Where should a period be placed? At which point does one "no longer need" [to keep going]? Is it when the other is in danger, when he is unfaithful to himself, when he runs out of steam? "You have to stand by your friends, especially if they are wrong"—this French proverb applies nowhere more so than in marriage! When one partner ravages his soul, is not the other one called all the more to go to battle with him for his sake? Is this obligation rescinded by the separation that may have become necessary? Quite to the contrary. The door must remain open—"soluble" divorce slams the door closed to this forever. If the other one does not come back, the one who remains behind will accompany the one who has departed with prayer and, most importantly, with atonement: responsible for him or her until death.

I understood this for the first time—and ever since then—when an abandoned, divorced woman, whose husband had succumbed to a stronger fascination

84 In German, the verbs translated here as "un-folds" and "un-furls" are *ent-faltet* and *ent-wickelt*, respectively, with a hyphen added by Görres to emphasize the prefix. The German prefix *ent-* can indicate the beginning of something.

after a few short years of happiness, said to me: "Now I have to be faithful for two." She persevered in this impeccably for over forty years until his death.

72

But who can handle that? Love that is mortally wounded, fondness that is extinguished, trust that is violated? Only covenant, law, and grace.

73

They tell us, however: Jesus did not *want* any law.[85] First of all, it is a perversion to ascribe anything to Him. At most, He articulated prophetic commands in the most general terms. His pronouncement on divorce is in the Sermon on the Mount; it is adjacent to the prohibition

85 Görres is paraphrasing Hotz's article here. Hotz quotes a position paper from 1969 of the Lutheran church (*Evangelische Kirche*) in Germany, according to which the Sermon on the Mount "does not contain instructions for legal practice, but a new ethos that cannot be grasped by the standards of legal discussion and decision." Hotz, "Wiederverheiratung Geschiedener in der Kirche?," 212. And Hotz argues, "There is no doctrine of marriage in the NT [New Testament]. The Synoptics see marriage in terms of the coming reign of God, while the Epistles look more at the concrete situation of the Church. It follows that it is inadmissible to detach the statements on marriage in the NT from their context and to use them unseen as legal or moral prescriptions. When, for example, in Mt [Matthew] 5:31 and following Jesus' prohibition of divorce appears in the Sermon on the Mount, then it must be judged in the same way as the other prohibitions of the Sermon on the Mount (prohibition of swearing, prohibition of retaliation), namely as calls to free, radical following of Jesus, but not as legal norms." Hotz, "Wiederverheiratung Geschiedener in der Kirche?," 214.

of oaths and the command to turn the other cheek.[86] Why did the Church make a law out of this?

We pose the question the other way around: Why did the Church, why *did* the Spirit, who left the other two directives "free-floating" and thus up to the striving of believers for perfection, write this very statement on an iron slab and solidify it more and more? Does not this fact alone show us the enormous importance and urgency of this? Nor, with the best will in the world, can I find any prophetic images of the future in the continually repeated, succinct diagnosis: he "divorces his wife."[87] This is spoken to those listening and asking questions here and now, not for vague, messianic, eschatological futures.[88] He spoke about this extensively in other places, as well.

"Jesus," one man would have us believe, "understands marriage to be an innermost attitude . . . which does not permit any intrusive legal regulation from the outside, in any case, can never be identical with that." "Marriage" becomes an indefinable phenomenon in the atmosphere between two people, something that one has or does not have, regarding the existence of which

86 Matthew 5:31–39. Hotz writes: "Protestant theologians usually interpret the marriage commandment in the context of the intention of the Sermon on the Mount: 'an ideal for preaching' takes the place of casuistic interpretation of the law." Hotz, "Wiederverheiratung Geschiedener in der Kirche?," 216; see also, 214.

87 Matthew 5:32.

88 Hotz, by contrast, writes, "The Synoptic" Gospels "see marriage in terms of the coming reign of God." And he says, "It is impossible to transfer the New Testament statements unmediated into our time." Hotz, "Wiederverheiratung Geschiedener in der Kirche?," 214. Similarly, see Heinz-Dietrich Wendland, *Botschaft an die soziale Welt*, 119.

only those involved can decide (with the exception, of course, of certain psychology specialists who are "omniscient" and "infallible" in human terms). And where this intangible element disappears, there is nothing left that anyone can still adjudicate. If Jesus had meant this, if those hearing Him had understood His words this way, why then the alarmed reaction of the disciples: "If such is the case of a man with his wife, it is not expedient to marry" (Matthew 19:10)!? (Weizäcker translates "the case" (*die Sache*) [in this verse] as "the right" (*das Recht*)!)[89] With a magic wand, that interpretation would have eliminated all practical problems. How, if it were applied, would there be any adultery after the situation in which a marriage has "lost its flavor"?

And *if* He *had*—just for the sake of discussion—meant it at the time only as prophecy, have *we* not had enough in time in this matter to fulfill it? And *if* the Gospel writers *had* understood it that way—which is pure hypothesis, without any trace of "proof"!—who can, who should even want to, reduce the overall development of the Church to the understanding of "back then," even if it could be reproduced for us? Squeezing the plant back into the mustard seed, the living, mature human back into the embryo? The ever-present Lord speaks to us as well—not only to the Apostles; it is, also, Him speaking in "synchronicity," which so occupied

89 *Das Neue Testament*, trans. Carl von Weizsäcker, 35. "Das Recht" could also be translated as "justice" or even as "due" (as in "what is due") or "privilege."

Kierkegaard and which Guardini recognized in the Church: "He who hears you hears me."[90]

74

But here, too, does not the law, Church law, beget sins? We know about the instability of contemporaries; they know it themselves. Is it not presumptuous to promise loyalty forever? Did we—even the youngest—not go through so much rupture and upheaval that we can no longer believe in anything abiding? Do the younger ones even know of a living role model for abiding? Why, of all things, should the most changeable thing that exists, the human heart, be excluded or, perhaps even more seriously, want to be exempt [from changing]? Who would dare to do that? No one, other than with a "so help me God."

75

Here, a central reality that we are on the verge of suppressing must be called to mind: namely, the importance of the Church *wedding*.

In contrast to kinship-marriage, as we have already mentioned, the Church had to elevate the sole binding power of the personal "yes." In our century, which began with considerable legal formalism, the first youth renewal in the [19]20s emphasized with passion that *we* give the sacrament to each other, not

90 Luke 10:16.

the priest to us. With the familiar one-sidedness of the joy of discovering something new, the role of the priest was soon reduced to being a kind of pastoral registrar or wedding witness. And since the [state] registry office has actually taken over the registration function of Church records, anymore, the wedding ceremony seems only to provide a "ceremonial setting" for the espousal—a "moment of ambiance." But that is far too little; it completely obscures the spiritual function of the priest at the wedding. This construes it minimalistically as in the highly insufficient, in my view, explanation in the *Lexikon für Kirche und Theologie* (*Encyclopedia for Church and Theology*): "He is [only] a qualified assistant to clarify the spiritual and ecclesial substance of the marriage."[91] This is not *action.*

The priest is *also* a witness to the wedding. But his conduct differs significantly from that of other witnesses and the registry office. He not only enquires about, not only listens, to the declaration of intent, rather: "In the name of the Church *confirmo* (*I confirm*) and I bless this covenant." *Confirmare,* which is unfortunately made empty and flat in translation [into German] with "*bestätigen*" ("confirm") as one would for the receipt of a package or payment. *Confirmo* means: I make firm, I strengthen, I *make* it durable and steadfast. I—that is, the Church acting in her office as Christ, who is present. This is more than just a friendly congratulation from the minister. Blessing is a communication of

91 Johannes Petrus Michael, "Ehe," 3:682. At the beginning of this sentence, Görres writes, in quotation marks, "Er sei ein . . ." This sentence in the text of this article instead begins, "Der Priester ist nur ein . . ."

strength—the inflowing power of inception, multiplication, and growth; it is instituted by the Church as the presence of grace for this inchoate covenant. What a shame that we do not have *the laying on of hands* like the Reformed Christians as a sign of the transmission of spiritual power! Maybe it is hiding in the wrapping of the wedding couple's hands with the stole? But we should know. And so should the priests, too.

Something here joins that which is human. Indeed, it is something that our consideration of this has not yet caught up with.

The Byzantine wedding rite expresses it most clearly: "God, priest of the mystical and immaculate marriage covenant . . . extend your hand, O Lord, *now* and marry your servant and your maid, because it is from you that the woman is joined to the man." The Reformed wedding ritual is actually far more "Catholic" than ours—the exchange of rings takes place only *after* the blessing and "indicates that the action of the *church* genuinely constitutes marriage." "The blessing forms the climax of the service and gives the confidence that God will give the promised grace and accompany their life together."

This goes far beyond the couple's consent of "yes." Here, something "happens" over which they have no power. Here, something is granted to them and their covenant on which—reasonably, one would like to say—the couple can rely first of all, more than on feeling, intent, or the strength of character.

76

But if we invoke the liturgical example of the Reformed and Eastern Christians, why only here and not in the fact that both acknowledge and practice "real" divorce, that is, with the right to second marriage? Again and again, the address of [Archbishop Zoghby] at the [Second Vatican] Council for those divorced innocently to have the freedom to marry is invoked today, and this is one of the strongest arguments of the advocates for this.[92]

But one can assure oneself from relevant accounts precisely from Reformed and Orthodox authors that this is *not at all* taken for granted, least of all as exemplary, in this particular circumstance among them

92 There may be an error at this point in the German text. Görres refers to "the address of Patriarch Maximos" but it appears she is referring not to a speech by Melkite Patriarch Maximos IV Sayegh but rather by Archbishop Elias Zoghby, the Greek Melkite Patriarchal Vicar for Egypt and the Sudan, under Patriarch Maximos, at the Second Vatican Council on September 29, 1965, in which Archbishop Zoghby spoke about "the problem of the innocent spouse who, in the prime of life and through no fault of his or her own, is left alone through the other spouse's fault." He suggested the Church should, as an exception to its teaching on the indissolubility of marriage, allow divorce and remarriage in such situations, and asked, "Can the Church in this case offer only an exceptional solution that it knows is meant only for exceptional persons?" In response, on October 2, 1965, Patriarch Maximos in an interview with *La Croix* newspaper commented on Archbishop Zoghby's intervention and provided some "clarifications": "With respect to the heart of the problem, the Church must hold fast to the indissolubility of marriage, for, even though in certain cases the innocent spouse is sorely tried because of this law, the whole of family life would be shaken and ruined without this law. Moreover, if divorce in the strict sense were to be allowed on the grounds of adultery, nothing would be easier for less conscientious spouses than to create this cause." Archbishop Zoghby, in turn, raised the issue again on October 4, 1965. Patriarch of Antioch Maximos, *The Melkite Church at the Council*, Chapter 15.

(for example, in the extensive anthology on marriage: *Revue de Droit Canonique* Tome XXI No. 1–4, "Le Lien Matrimonial," 1971, Université de Strasbourg).[93] The authors downright squirm with apologies and justifications. They compete with each other in emphasizing how much their *doctrines* recognized and always proclaimed Christ's absolute prohibition of divorce and His stipulation about adultery for a second wedding, and how much the practice [of divorce with allowance for remarriage] was an importunate—even hated—compromise. They are fully aware of the contradiction. In the Eastern Church, an emperor, not a patriarch, inserted this "right" into the church canons. The state imposed it on the church because the unbelieving state grants divorces for marriages and permits remarriage, but the latter cannot take place without a church wedding. The [Eastern] Church does not dissolve the marriage; it only takes note of divorce. Such a second marriage is no longer a "mysterion" (a sacrament); the married couple is denied the crown and canopy decorations of the first wedding, the priest is not allowed to attend the wedding feast, etc. Even the rite of a "second" marriage is more penitence than anything else: "You know about the weakness of human nature . . . you forgave Rahab the prostitute and accepted the conversion of the tax collector . . . Grant them [the couple] the tears of the sinner, the confession of the thief because they cannot

93 There appears to be a typographical error in the German edition which reads *Le Lieu Matrimonial*. The title of this volume is *Le Lien Matrimonial*, that is, *The Marriage Bond*.

bear the heat . . . of the day and the fire in the flesh."[94] This is not exactly applause and celebration.

77

The Greeks call this practice *oikonomia*—that is, so to speak, the moment of "distribution," the allocation—probably here of blessing and the sacrament. (In the Eastern church, the *priest*, not the couple, bestows the sacrament of marriage!) The *oikonomia* is applied mercy, when the strictness of the law knows no way out.

The authors from the Reformed church also squirm when they need to justify their practice; they also perceive it as problematic. That is how it is in the extensive Strasbourg anthology [of the *Revue de Droit Canonique*]. The regional Lutheran churches today have distanced themselves far from the opinion of Luther (which the Council of Trent condemned), who said that "every Christian and spouse can judge for himself or herself whether and when their marriage is dissolved, and no ecclesiastical authority may lawfully intervene."[95] It is no longer possible for every pastor to comply with the request of the divorced for a second marriage at

94 See, for comparison, the Greek "Order for a Second Marriage": "Thou who knowest the infirmity of man's nature, who formed it and made it, who didst forgive Rahab the harlot," and accept the repentance of the Publican . . . give to them the Publican's conversion, the Harlot's tears." Joel Foote Bingham, *Christian Marriage*, 260–61. Regarding forgiveness of Rahab, see Hebrews 11:31 and James 2:25; regarding the publican, see Luke 18:13; regarding the harlot's tears, see Luke 7:37–38.

95 This may be a paraphrase from "The Babylonian Captivity of the Church." See Martin Luther, *Three Treatises*, 223–224.

will, but only a committee chaired by the regional bishop may permit such an exception after the strictest examination. A remarkable step in the direction of Catholic austerity since my youth, when in Austria the average opinion on the difference between Catholics and Protestants was neither in "faith or works," nor even in the papacy and veneration of saints, but very simply: "The others are allowed to marry as often as they want!" And the remarriage of the divorced was the most common reason to convert to another confession. Similarly, among the Greeks one reads:

The second marriage means "that God's grace *may* be called down on the couple, but it does not mean that the divorce is approved. Divorce is the fruit of sin and must be recognized as such . . . but *we have to acknowledge its consequences*."

This exactly is what the Latin Church does as well—only with different repercussions.

78

And *if* our Church differs on this point from the Eastern as well as the Reformation churches: Why should we assume that she is wrong specifically here and has to align herself to them? It could very well be an indication that, specifically in this, by the guidance of the Holy Spirit, she was able to maintain greater loyalty to the Word of God, with fewer concessions to the ever-pressing demand and logic of the "world" in the Johannine sense, which are so formidable.

79

This is so at least in the fidelity of *doctrine* and *general* practice. It is apparent in the Roman Catholic Church that, in individual cases, this practice was, time and again, uneven. But if, somewhere, at some point, a priest has demonstrably broken the seal of confession, can one then conclude that everyone should just take it less seriously? It borders on the grimly comical how all the discordant behavior of a Carolingian bishop, a pope in the Hohenstaufen era, who dissolved a marriage bond, was conceding to a deplorable *custom* of his era—perhaps under pressure from a powerful person?—yet is now recommended to the Church of today as a shining example. And this is from people who ignore the solemn encyclical *Humanae vitae* as a private opinion of Montini [Pope Paul VI] that is not binding on anyone but himself.

Why should [Pope] Nicholas I or Alexander III suddenly be more "infallible" than [Pope] Pius XII or Paul VI?

80

But another circumstance is far more serious.

The conscience of *believers* confronts an issue in today's official annulment practice with growing discomfort: the annulment of marriages, even of long-standing ones with children, due to *mere paperwork errors* at the wedding. With all due respect for the meaning and weightiness of the wedding: Who can accept this; who can take it seriously?

It seems rather certain that it is never really just a matter of *pure* paperwork errors that neither of them ever realized beforehand. Rather, the errors are suddenly fished up because someone wants to marry someone else. Even the person who has married invalidly while completely willing to marry is not simply free to choose between having his marriage annulled *or* made valid (*convalidated*). First, one would be *obliged* to attempt remediation; the alternative appears as a backhanded legal trick so that one can achieve nothing other than what is otherwise simply called divorce with a legal license. And who should not assume where there was a genuine paperwork error at the beginning that it might not have been made up for in subsequent normal married life, when possible, with children, through the "provision of the Church," *Ecclesia supplet*, by the sacred consummation, the sacramentality of which cannot be erased by the mere discovery of a paperwork error made years ago?

Such occurrences—known to many—if they do not make the faith of the ordinary, obedient believer in indissolubility difficult, then they at least severely strain his trust in the Church in this regard.

The situation is similar in dealing with the Pauline Privilege.[96] I cannot hide the fact that the two cases I know of appear to be highly contestable. Here and there are probably priests, mostly individuals, who, desperate

96 See 1 Corinthians 7:12–17.

for help, perhaps after long deliberation, decide that a little duplicity is the lesser evil compared to hardship, and that with some skill, one could "legally" pull it off—who would notice? Nothing could be of less concern, or even more welcome, to the couple, and there are hardly any observers, so the risk of outrage is low. We do not want to judge such a decision; God may count it as an act of love. Actually, it would correspond precisely to what the Greek [Orthodox] practice as *oikonomia* if it were an explicit act of *mercy*. But the *legalistic* fiction in this is what is confusing and destroys trust. *This*, more so than her strictness, harms the credibility of the Church.

Nietzsche is right once again about "folly that happens out of pity."[97]

In these three matters (the third is the monks getting married), one can only seriously hope and ask that the practice be tightened, not made laxer, in order for credibility to return.

81

At the same time, we have to ask, hope, and urge that those responsible be bolder and more thorough, in practice, regarding *annulment due to a lack of will to be married*. This, in no way, means softer. A sharp distinction must be made here.

97 Görres is paraphrasing. Nietzsche writes, "Their spirit was drowned in their pity; and when they were swollen and overswollen with pity, it was always a great folly that swam on top." Nietzsche, *Thus Spoke Zarathustra*, 92.

82

There are probably many cases of *sham-marriages*. Not those resourceful couples—who do exist—who incorporate deliberate paperwork errors from the start so that they can later leave for a new marriage happily with a clear conscience. Rather, what is simpler and more common is that very many contemporaries, including those who are baptized, even believers or those who consider themselves to be believers, do *not*, in fact, have the threefold will to fertility, exclusivity, and duration until death, which, according to Church doctrine, alone creates the actual indissolubility of the marriage covenant. In practice, they marry on a trial basis, with the caveat perhaps unspoken but in their hearts: "Let us make an honest effort—and if things go wrong, we are decent enough to give the other person a new chance." Who can judge them? They have never seen or learned otherwise. With young women who have been abandoned by their husbands after a short time, it is now often a matter of such sham-marriages: one should encourage them in this circumstance to move on. Not because leaving a woman (or vice versa), especially with a child, is not clearly a base thing—even base things have to be forgiven in marriage—but because they really are not in the bond of marriage and, therefore, after civil divorce, would not have to forgo a later marriage.

83

But what are people supposed to do, well-meaning nominal or marginal Catholics, who simply do not have the threefold will for marriage because they were never brought up for this, do not know any credible models, and perhaps hear about this for the first time in marriage preparation? For many, this may serve as something like a revelation of new possibilities and a real "conversion" to this path that is offered. Such an experience could be deepened and strengthened by a kind of "engagement novitiate." But anyone who is *not* able or does *not* want this should be *warned* expressly and emphatically against a Church wedding. They could only accept it hypocritically. Their "I do" would be a deliberate lie, and they would not be able to meet the unalterable demands of Christian, sacramental marriage any more than the consequences of failure, that is, a divorce.

What, then, should they do? Good advice here is truly precious. They—and even more so their parents—should muster the *courage to have a civil marriage*, cognizant of what they are doing, not out of immature defiance nor in the self-deception that this is actually the same just without ecclesial "magic." As long as they remain in their "trial-marriage" *posture*, a civil marriage would actually be nothing other than a trial-marriage, that is, a stabilized nonmarital relationship, even if legally recognized [by the state]. For this reason alone, the Church could never recognize civil marriages *en masse* as valid. On the other hand, such couples honestly want the *trial* to be permanent; if they have lived together before, they want to be brought "in order." Here, it should be seriously considered whether a partnership structure has, in fact, already developed, which looks more like ancient concubinage than Christian marriage. It would be a strange intermediate situation, civilly legal, especially with regard to the children, objectively not a sacramental covenant, *subjectively not necessarily and in all cases* a "sinful relationship"; somehow (I know how inadequate this statement is!) for the unwed, with regret, but still to be tolerated and to be formed so that they may be up to marriage. But is cohabitation-"marriage" not actually something quite like this? The Church wedding, however, should be reserved for those who are committed to accept all of its implications in full, especially sacramentality. An extraordinarily subtle and prudent pastoral differentiation would be necessary here; we certainly know how dreamlike it sounds. But does one not have to wish and strive for that which is rare and difficult so that it becomes a reality?

84

The genuinely broken marriages that were not sham-marriages are a different matter.

One speaks of the "breakdown" the way one speaks of a mysterious plague that overcomes a marriage unexpectedly and incurably, which one regrets just as one regrets bad luck, and excuses as an accident and as something onto which one can shower compassion, as with a misfortune. In fact, marital breakdown *is* the fruit of sin, of many, long, desired, and known, cherished and cultivated sins on at least one side. It is based mostly on adultery.

(Who wants to determine the "distribution of guilt"? Through coldness, jealousy, exploitation of others, many "decent" women drove their husbands away; by their roughness, domination, and ruthlessness, many honorable men have handed over their wives to the first sensitive and well-mannered man she meets.) English studies show that so-called "divorce by mutual consent" is broached by *one* partner in nine out of ten cases; the other gives way, often in a thousand torments. In divorces, among those aged forty to fifty, 80 percent of all cases involve men who have found a younger partner. The majority of the women abandoned in this way remain "single."

85

People appeal to the Church as a sign of forgiveness, as a custodian of mercy, who should accept these people who have "failed" in order to comfort them, to "speak honestly" and thereby affirm them. This is curious. This tacitly presupposes that the death of a marriage is an elemental process, such as an earthquake or a typhoon, beyond human defense; one can only clear up the rubble afterward. In reality, a large share of broken marriages would have been healed if as much energy and intelligence had been put into healing as subsequently goes into getting out. The love that matters in *marriage* is mostly dependent on will and effort. What the ancients called *amor complacentiae* (love arising from attraction) and *amor concupiscentiae* (love arising from desire)—"you please me" and "you are the one I want"—start from the object [you], but *amor benevolentiae* (love arising from benevolence), "I treat you well," starts from the subject [I].

Rapture and desire for possession are, admittedly, the most prevalent types of experience. But here, too, "one often exalts brilliant actions and qualities, without which the moral world could very well exist, while the elements of them and their beauty and indispensability get overlooked and are therefore not sufficiently cultivated" (Alban Stolz).[98] Emphasis on "cultivate": because this love needs constant gardener-like care to thrive, bloom, and bear fruit. But if someone has neither watered nor fertilized his plants, can he then complain about them withering as an incomprehensible injustice that is happening to him?

Would the pastoral duty not be above *all* to counsel the endangered marriages—which are also a part of the Church, actually a most critical part as a sign of the Covenant of God and Christ—with all means and powers to ask that *they themselves be signs of forgiveness*, of mutual forgiveness seventy-times-seven, of peace, mercy, and reconciliation? And if they do not want this? When it is too late? Then the Church has to say what is at hand.

98 Alban Stolz, *Spanisches für die gebildete Welt,* 128. Translation by Bryson.

86

So many are upset that the Church "discriminates" too *little*, that she denounces and condemns too little in political and social realms, often on issues that are not directly her domain. In some respects, the critics are right. They, in particular, should not demand that the Church remain silent about other corruptions by which the world will perish just as surely.

If the Church had made it a maxim always to follow the trends of the era in respect to approvals and contempt, we would still have blood feuds, tribal justice over death and life, duels, no rights for prisoners, etc. Now, at least, these things happen without her approval. And where, over the centuries, she has actually adapted to existing severely deplorable customs: to financial corruption in the awarding of offices, witch-hunts, torture, and slavery—are these not scars on her history?

The Church should adapt to the "changed circumstances" [they say]—to the general mentality; this is suspiciously reminiscent of the "sound sense of the people," which sanctioned Jew-baiting and murder of invalids in the Nazi era.

Should she give approval for adultery, abortion, and homosexual chaos today because the state and society have become "permissive"?

87

Who even still understands what adultery *really* is, the almost "mystical" sin, the actual symbol for all betrayal of God Himself? In the Old Testament, both died as criminals;[99] incidentally, this is still so in Saudi Arabia. In the early Church, the penitents were still punished with lifelong penance—that is, exclusion from the Eucharist, and in the Middle Ages with years of extra fasting. In any case, marriage between the adulterer and the guilty partner was always considered a new crime. This guilt was equivalent to the "capital sins" of murder and apostasy.

Fairy tales from ancient times! The complicity of public opinion today is terrible. When people said "liquidate" for murders and "organize" for stealing and fraud, decent people were outraged by the "dictionary of the unhuman."[100] The terms "little friend" and "constant companion" camouflage adultery so benevolently that out of embarrassment one already has to avoid the words "boyfriend" and "girlfriend." Should the Church go along? Is it unfair discrimination if she does not do so?

88

Incidentally, today, socially, very different people are discriminated against: parents with many children—the father viewed as a criminal, the mother as

99 See Leviticus 20:10 and Deuteronomy 22:22.

100 Following the Second World War, those speaking German associated the phrase "dictionary of the unhuman" with the euphemisms developed by the Nazi regime. This vocabulary was the subject of a well-known book published in 1957: Adolf Sternberger, Gerhard Storz, and W. E. Suskind, eds., *Aus dem Wörterbuch des Unmenschen*. The word I translate as "unhuman" (*Unmensch*), could also be translated as brute, ogre, monster, or hellkite.

stupid, both as crazy; innocent girls as infantile, cowardly, or abnormal; chaste young men as stupid and perverted; in some circles, even happy young married couples who are still so bourgeois as to be loyal to each other, and, of course, priests who still dare to call a spade a spade in these matters are viewed as zealots and tyrants of conscience. No one gets upset about such discrimination.

89

A truism: condemning an act, establishing something as a breach of the law does not condemn a person or deny that he has any lovable qualities. One reads "hate the sin, love the sinner" already in Augustine.[101] It is a childish notion that "sinners" should also be repulsive villains. *Corruptio optimi pessima* (there is nothing worse than the corruption of the best).

How foolish is the popular plea: "But there are such lovely, upright, and dear people among them!" Since when would those qualities ever keep people from sinning! It is as if with battleships, one wanted to "moor the vessel with a thread of silk,"[102] as Newman said.

101 St. Augustine writes, "with love for the person and hatred for the sin." Augustine of Hippo, "Rule," in George Lawless, *Augustine of Hippo and His Monastic Rule*, 93 and 114.

102 Newman writes, "Quarry the granite rock with razors, or moor the vessel with a thread of silk; then you may hope with such keen and delicate instruments as human knowledge and human reason to contend against those giants, the passion and the pride of man." John Henry Newman, *The Idea of a University*, 121.

90

There is hardly a more idiotic sentimental slogan than "understanding everything means forgiving everything." First, as if *I* had to forgive someone else's sins that did not affect me. Second, as if one could forgive something other *than* a sin. Third, as if the objective weight of a sin would be erased by my personal understanding and consent. Fourth, [as if] the deeper I understand a sin, the more I have to reject it. It is incredible how this tactical sentimentality thrives. "Can one handle this in the long run, to see others go to communion and not to be allowed to go? In this second marriage, these spouses have now become parents, whose children are preparing for first communion and who now ask: 'Father, mother, why don't you go [to communion]?'—is the Church not too strict here?"

Or what smacks even worse:

"Extended life expectancy makes it harder for a man today; once, he could count on his wife quickly dying at childbirth and that he could legitimately get himself a little something new and fresh several times. Today, the poor man sometimes has to endure thirty or forty years with his old wife—what an impertinence! How excusable a little infidelity would be!" This, formulated, of course more politely, is what we read in an article by a professor of Catholic morality.

Or brotherly pity turns to the one who destroyed the marriage: How does it come to be that he or she has to abide the poor adulterer whom he or she already made so happy? Is not their mutual love—as love—beautiful and strong and, therefore, worth encouraging? In "academic" terms, this means:

"If marriage as love = destroying a shared life, there is no longer a sacrament because the sacrament comes into being in married life and is not something added." In this case, the *new lovers* have *a right* to marry. They are only refused on the premise that the first spouse still has rights. "But this right has actually lost its meaning. . . . [I]ndeed, it would be an *immoral right* because a third party has now emerged, to whom there is a *moral* obligation of love, loyalty, and care." In other words: New love makes the existing marriage—not the new relationship—immoral. Adulterers have always argued this way in kitschy romance novels. The surprise today is that one can read this from the pen of theologians.

One thinks of Goethe: "There is nothing more dangerous than a conversation which takes liberties and treats as usual, commonplace, or even praiseworthy a situation which is reprehensible or half reprehensible; and surely it must be deemed dangerous whenever the marriage bond is belittled in that way."[103] We really have come this far.

For this very reason, he is, unfortunately, right that "in confusions of a moral kind educated people are harder to assist than uneducated."[104]

103 Goethe, *Elective Affinities*, 68.

104 Goethe, *Elective Affinities*, 109.

91

Is it just, is it brotherly, by tacit complicity, by strengthening false hopes, to deprive the perhaps not a few people who still allow themselves to be kept from sin by "discriminating" against it of their last support of conscience and to let them slide, where a healing effort to pull oneself together would still be possible? Should we deprive them of all courage to resist by offering the adulterous partner the bonus of a happy and rehabilitated marriage with the marriage-wrecker? The person who knows that he has to stay in his house tries promptly, that is, early on, to repair small damages. The person who already has a nicer place to live in sight will neglect the first one *on purpose* to have sufficient reasons for moving out early.

No one has ever been helped by being confirmed and reinforced in their iniquity. Those who confirm or reinforce another in his iniquity even block the path of reflection, insight, and repentance. They do not help the other person, but rather deepen his delusion that "happiness" is more important than "salvation," that our "right to happiness" outclasses God's right to our obedience.

92

Which Christian can justify such a thing in someone else's marriage? And how could the Church combine this with the fact that being the proclaimer of the message of God is her only right to exist?

93

J. H. Newman saw the Church, above all, as the great prophet,[105] the penitent prophet on earth, who is responsible for the Truth of God, the Law of God, she who must call sin by its name and may not say "peace, peace" where there is none.[106] This is a formidable but unavoidable mandate of the pastoral office. "If *I* say to the wicked, 'You shall surely die,' and you give him no warning . . . that wicked man shall die in his iniquity; but his blood I will require at your hand. But if you warn the wicked, and he does not turn from his wickedness, . . . he shall die in his iniquity; but you will have saved your life."[107]

"Merciful" recognition by the Church would mean:

1. A second marriage becomes, so to speak, the reward of a successful, long enough, tenacious enough, perseverance in adultery. The guilty may now, without repentance, with a so-called clear conscience—after all, he has the blessing of the Church!—happily continue on the chosen path with his marriage-wrecking partner.
2. The previously innocent partner is publicly encouraged to copy the guilt of the former, to repeat it, so that both have irrevocably destroyed reconciliation.

105 See, for example, John Henry Newman, *Lectures on the Prophetical Office of the Church.*

106 See Jeremiah 8:11.

107 Ezekiel 3:18–19.

From this should come salvation for both and "credibility" for the Church.[108]

94

Ecclesiastical "discrimination" consists of barring a person from the sacraments. Everyone knows that even the *secret* adulterer, the seducer is excluded from receiving the Eucharist and can only receive the sacrament of penance if he or she is ready to give up that state (which, unfortunately, it seems not all confessors know or seem to take seriously). In the second marriage, one now makes his condition *public* and declares that he *wants* to remain in it. Should that be a reason to remove the previous exclusion from the Eucharist? Strange logic! As for that which excludes people from the altar when it occurs occasionally, should it become guiltless when it becomes a permanent condition?

Can whoever stands consciously, decisively, and before the world outside the law of the Church, in a matter which she expressly identifies in faith with God's command, whoever solemnly, publicly, and *in perpetuity* declares obedience to her—can he really, honestly, and with a clear conscience want to come to the "table of unity," which presents the visible bond of

108 Regarding "credibility," Hotz writes, "Analogous to the origin of the New Testament statements on the indissolubility of marriage, in which a general aspirational commandment [*Zielgebot*] is confronted with the situation of the congregation under the question of the credible realization of the Kingdom of God, the establishment of rules today should also be based on both the commandment [*Gebot*] of Christ and the changed spiritual and social situation of the congregation and its members." Hotz, 8.

the children united in faith, love, *and obedience* to the Church? We, who always keep [the phrase] "the Church of sinners" on the tip of our tongues, forget too easily that sin and penance belong together, and forgiveness can only be called for when there is a will to *repent*. Consider that penance in the Church was once taken so gravely, seriously in a physical sense, that there was a separate, recognizable state of the penitents!!

Has the Church in this way really created "a caste of public sinners"? Or do not those very people place themselves in their sin, through their sin, in a relatively public position that no one can take away from them, by the nature of the thing?

After all, accepting the consequences of a freely chosen decision is part of human dignity, even if someone chooses to be guilty.

95

But we hear the response that people used to feel guilt. Today, at least in these matters, they feel none. You cannot want to force them to act against their own feelings. Now, this is a very interesting point.

It is precisely here that the lawbreaker often has an uncanny keen sensitivity. Why else does he want to be "justified" at all costs?

It is distressing to see how the very people who openly rebel against the precept of the Church do not want to accept it as a Commandment from God and insist proudly on this as proof of their maturity—how at the same time they beg for recognition and confirmation *through* the law; they want to force it and fool it!

Today, we take a certain pride in emphasizing that the Church is a church of sinners. But who wants to exemplify this himself? It is very strange: this attitude is especially typical of the whole complex of sexuality, in which people want to feel and declare they are most free. At the same time, nowhere do they place more value on "rehabilitation" in the face of despised morality. The same attitude was also evident in the ferocious ruckus over *Humanae vitae*. Female protestors, in particular, were most annoyed—not about the prohibitions, but that "failure due to weakness" should also still be confessed *and* "treated with compassion." "How can the pope dare to assume that modern people could succumb to weakness in bed instead of always acting deliberately with unfettered responsibility!!" This seemed to be the core insult.

It is precisely in the area where every accusation is fended off most stridently that one is most sensitive to innuendo because one presumes that in this regard, one always has to be "on the up and up" to be right.

Humans want to do what suits them. They, therefore, reduce the law of the Church to pure human hocus-pocus—but, in the end, she should "grant" they are "right."

"The woman always wants to be right; the man never wants to be wrong," said a clever friend to me. This also applies here. This shows, strangely, that even people who insist on autonomy know that they cannot be "right" if one does not "*grant*" that they are "right" at the same time.

96

"Contradictions go to make up human destiny, and it was not until our own era, with its morbid hyperaesthesia of the self and its gross egalitarianism, that it was found to be a matter for indignation and scandal" and for the demand *that the exception should become the norm* (Thibon).[109]

But legality is not the only human good. Situations can even have a deep and distinct dignity, which the believer, in particular, appreciates with sympathy and awe, even if we do not quite adopt the Spanish proverb: "Do what you like, pay the price, and God will be satisfied."[110]

For someone who encounters a very great love, an existential love that conflicts with his marriage—and that happens—the Church, Thibon says, provides a tremendous *choice*: either heroic renunciation (out of awareness of the sacrament, the eschatological dimension of marriage, and God's Will in the law) or *openly* break the law and endure all the responsibilities, consequences, and suffering. "There is something worse than sin: the *fraudulent* desire to win two prizes at a single throw: to reap the pleasure of sin and the advantages of virtue, the intoxication of anarchy and

109 Gustave Thibon, *Love at the Crossroads*, 112–13.

110 Thibon, *Love at the Crossroads*, 118–19.

the benefits of law and order. In this gamble, everything noble and profound still left in the sin evaporates at once."[111] We endorse this wholeheartedly. It is really a deceptive maneuver, which contradicts the most basic common sense. One cannot have his cake and eat it, too. One cannot, as an Indian saying goes, roast half the chicken and expect eggs from the other half.

97

Here, too, situations and attitudes differ considerably. In addition to the unrepentant, stubborn and, so to speak, triumphant adulterer who has successfully fought through his demand against the Church for legal status and happiness and is now still making demands, there are, in the immense confusion of our conditions, also people of goodwill —and not a few—who, *subjectively innocent in objectively wrong relationships,* land in hopeless dead ends.

For example, out of love and pity, a young woman marries a man with young children whose wife has run away. Or a woman who had to remove an alcoholic, violent husband for the sake of the children has an indispensable worker on the farm who wants to marry her. Or two who have been abandoned meet as colleagues and find each other entirely complementary.

Some do not even understand that they are still bound, that one cannot be married to two living people just because the one who disappeared has faded into

111 Thibon, *Love at the Crossroads,* 119. Italics added by Görres.

an unpleasant memory; they cannot see beyond what is visible. Who wants to throw the first stone? But who can rescind the fact that both *are* no longer free for a Christian marriage?

Others know or suspect, at least sometimes, that their lives are not in order. They may acknowledge in their hearts the right of the Church to command and prohibit, but with resignation, they are humbly aware that they can no longer bring about repentance, detachment, a "break up." Perhaps they also think they should not be allowed to do this because they have already taken on too much responsibility—children—and they are afraid of doing things worse than they have already done. They suffer in their predicament and would love to fix it—if only it were not so difficult. They do not demand rights, but rather mourn their failure. One can call this a toss-up, indecision. But such suffering detoxifies a lot that it cannot change.

Such a civil marriage can be a fair attempt made out of longing for the least disorderly order because circumstances cannot achieve full orderliness.

Such an attitude exists. It is by no means the presumptuousness of God's Mercy, which the old catechism places under the "sins that cry out to heaven," nor is it an excuse using situational ethics. Rather, it is very close to the *penitent's* attitude, and it may be a promising path to true penance.

In his large, unfortunately already forgotten, book on Dostoevsky's characters, Guardini has dealt very extensively with this attitude of the believing and pious sinner who *remains* in sin.[112] He suggested, admittedly somewhat hesitantly, that it might only be possible for Eastern people, with their more tender mind and vague will. It seems to me rather a simply human matter that does justice to the complexity of our existence. The sinner recognizes his condition, without glossing over it, as bondage and not something to boast about; he does not consider himself a martyr of injustice. Instead, he leaves it wholeheartedly to God to keep and guide him despite this, in ways that only He knows, which He already knows today, to lead this love out of confusion. In the meantime, he prepares for this day through prayer and humble consent through the atoning punishments in which there is already healing.

So much genuine devotion, loyalty, sacrifice, and selflessness is often invested in such circumstances—as much as in cohabitation-"marriage"!

The Church, in other sacraments, recognizes *sacramentum in voto* (sacrament of desire): baptism of desire, spiritual communion. One can probably ask whether in such cases a longing for proper and holy marriage it is not also what actually makes this special alliance a "means of grace" for the two—that is "sacramental"—although it is not classified this way according to the letter of the law. This is where the inseparable combination, especially in marriage, of inner and outer order, comes into play. We can confidently leave that to God, who has bound us to His Commandments and

112 Romano Guardini, *Der Mensch und der Glaube: Versuche über die religiöse Existenz in Dostojewskijs großen Romanen.*

outward signs, but He Himself, in His grace, is not bound to them. He can grant the *res sacramenti* (the reality of the sacrament) without the external sign.

God can make springs burst forth in the desert of an apparently incurable situation like they did for Hagar in a barren land.[113] From such soil, He can grow flowers that do not thrive even in many well-kept gardens. I even think that this condition could be seen as a peculiar *modern form of the state of penance* in the Church. It is also known that the penitent in front of the church door was by no means "discriminated" against; instead, the faithful who came to the celebration [of Mass] asked him to pray for them. Only, in this case, he is *hidden* from people, and this is as it should be. I could also imagine that in such cases, the [Apostolic] Penitentiary,[114] the secret *office of the grace* of the Church, would have a special leeway and that it would be possible that the bishops be involved in individual cases on the question of the admission to the sacraments. As is well known, Charles Péguy found himself in cohabitation with an unbaptized woman during his conversion. She threatened suicide if he baptized the children. He could not change the external situation—and a life of prayer and meditation was the fruit of it. Nobody sang of hope like he did.[115]

113 Genesis 16:1–16, Numbers 20:1–13.

114 The Apostolic Penitentiary is a tribunal of the Holy See with jurisdiction over the matters of the *forum internum* and indulgences.

115 One of Charles Péguy's most well-known poems was "The Portal of the Mystery of Hope."

98

Much discussed today in the case of broken marriages is the proposal to start by examining the partners' original "capacity for marriage" at the time of the wedding and to make the absence of such capacity the ground for annulment—more precisely: to do so for the partner who has become unpopular. This strikes me as highly problematic. A committee of psychologists (of course), doctors, lawyers, sociologists, and, last but not least, theologians, are supposed to decide. A "mental and psychological impotence to marry" is to be declared, which would carry as much weight as a physical reason. Such an examination may be justified *in the rarest of cases* where there is severe psychopathology, that is, where disillusionment in marriage is tantamount to *delusion in the person,* which is an old reason for annulment. But otherwise, just because of [marital] "breakdown"? Is that not too easy an escape route from guilt into determinism? Would it not be all too often too easy for those happy to divorce to bring up all sorts of mistakes, which they had always known about and taken into account, and then triumphantly bring them up in the event of a crisis? Would that be an iota better, more sincere, than a "paperwork error" in the proceeding?

How easy it would be to act for a while in such a way that a committee would have to certify an "anthropological disqualification from marriage"!

Here, "little reason" presumably usurps capacity to judge over and above "great reason";[116] the latter often brings together connections that no third party understands or needs, at least for those who are sensible. Well-known psychologists such as Albert Görres and [Viktor] E. Frankl tell us that analysis can follow the course of fate in retrospect: this is how it happened—but by no means how it *had* to be. There is always enough evidence that other circumstances have developed from similar, parallel factors. Here, freedom and grace are spirited away in favor of a fictitious causality. "Through you, I have become a different person" can be the result of highly problematic beginnings. "What God joined together"—how often is the inscrutable mystery of "approval" and "coincidence" at play here! Federer's autobiographical novel portrays the harrowing marriage of his parents—the drinking, vagabond artist father, and the strict, tough, forbearing wife: an impossible marriage that should never have come about according to reasonable criteria.[117] It produced an important poet, priest, and messenger of God, whose work has given many people rich gifts. It transformed

116 Görres may be referring to the concepts of "little reason" and "great reason" in Nietzsche's work *Thus Spoke Zarathustra*, a work she has quoted previously in this volume. Nietzsche writes, "The body is a great reason, a plurality with one sense, a war and a peace, a herd and a shepherd. An instrument of your body is also your little reason, my brother, which you call 'spirit'—a little instrument and toy of your great reason. 'I' you say, and are proud of the word. But greater is that in which you do not wish to have faith—your body and its great reason: that does not say 'I,' but does 'I.'" Nietzsche, *Thus Spoke Zarathustra*, 34; see also, 149, 166.

117 Görres is likely referring to: Heinrich Federer, *Am Fenster: Jugenderinnerungen*.

a small, rigid character into a great lover and gave a poor underachiever the inexpressible experience of an absolutely reliable, undying, divine patience and forgiveness. Would it have been better had all this not come to pass? And who does not know of such examples?

In such situations, moments of providence, personal fate, grace, and freedom play a part that no calculation can measure.

99

From this perspective, the question also seems very much to fall flat: "Can the biographical, often purely sociological *coincidence of being baptized* have the power to frustrate a whole human life"—because the Church declares the marriages of the baptized to be indissoluble? A counter-question: Can a Christian view his baptism as a coincidence and not as a personal election by God, the covenant between "God and me"? And if someone has no comprehension of this—is it less real? In such cases, is it not the duty of pastoral care to try to lead him to awareness of this, instead of helping him to completely suppress the meaning of this event in his life?

100

Talking about "frustration" as the only and necessary consequence of renunciation and sacrifice is simply unbecoming for Christians.[118] It implies the loss of two dimensions. First, the widespread experience that such a fate can lead to the greatest in human development, to the awakening, as it were, of new mental faculties, to the initiation of previously unknown deep forces—as is often the case with the sick, blind, crippled, orphaned, widowed, and displaced. Second, the *eschatological* dimension—"the acceptance, through grace, of a large or small part of the incomprehensibility of existence, carried out as participation in the fate of Jesus" ([Karl] Rahner)[119] and the firm hope in the promises of Christ that all life's tribulation is nothing compared to the coming glory.

101

With such considerations, the fierce controversy of *Church of the people or Church of the elite?* also comes into play subliminally. There is the dream of an ideal congregation, which consists only of intentional Christians who are all-in and active, who are committed, capable, and "credible," who offer a relatively perfect spectacle, with no one frustrated and all fully involved.

What utopianism! The Church will always have to be there for everyone, including for those from hither and thither who stumble,[120] to impose her law on those

118 Görres has a lengthy reflection on the value and role of renunciation in the Christian life in Chapter 3 of *On Marriage and on Being Single.*

119 Karl Rahner, "Die Zukunft der Orden in Welt und Kirche von heute," 352. Quotation translated by Bryson.

120 See Luke 14:21.

who do not keep it and on those who make her "lack credibility" in the eyes of the world. And from among them develop, again and again, unnoticed by the critics, true children of God, witnesses of His Mercy and His hidden Glory.

102

After a long roundabout way, we are back at the beginning, at the mystery. Marriage is a great mystery;[121] it will remain so and "He who is able to receive this let him receive it."[122]

121 See Ephesians 5:32.

122 Matthew 19:10.

REGISTER OF PERSONS

Abbreviations

CSsR Congregatio Sanctissimi Redemptoris (Congregation of the Sacred Redeemer, Redemptorist)

OSB Ordo Sancti Benedicti (Order of St. Benedict, Benedictine)

OP Ordo Praedicatorum (Order of Preachers, Dominican)

SJ Societas Iesu (Society of Jesus, Jesuit)

Abelard, Peter (1079–1142), scholastic philosopher, famous for his correspondence and relationship with Heloise; *see also* Heloise

Alexander III. *See* Popes

Alexius. *See* Saints

Aphrodite, Greek goddess associated with passion

Aquinas, Thomas. *See* Saints

Asmussen, Hans (1898–1968), German Lutheran pastor, friend of Ida Görres

Augustine. *See* Saints

Baader, Franz Xaver (1765–1841), German medical doctor, philosopher

von Balthasar, Hans Urs (1905–1988), Swiss Catholic priest, theologian, he and Görres corresponded

de Beauvoir, Simone (1908–1986), French philosopher, feminist

Benedict XVI. *See* Popes

Bernard of Clairvaux. *See* Saints.

Bertold of Regensburg (1200–1272), German Catholic preacher, Franciscan

Bovet, Theodor (1900–1976), Swiss Lutheran Protestant marriage counselor, neurologist

Chardin, Pierre Teilhard de, SJ (1881–1955), Catholic priest, paleontologist, controversial theologian

Cornelius Cornelii a Lapide, SJ (1567–1637), Catholic priest, Bible commentator

Coudenhove-Kalergi, Heinrich Count von (1859–1906), father of Ida Görres, Habsburg Empire diplomat

Coudenhove-Kalergi, Mitsuko Thekla Maria, Countess von (née Mitsuko Aoyama) (1874–1941), mother of Ida Görres, from Japan

Coudenhove–Kalergi, Richard Count von (1894 –1972), brother of Ida Görres, founder of the Pan-Europa movement

Doms, Herbert (1890–1977), German Catholic priest, author of works on moral theology

Dostoevsky, Fyodor (1821–1881), Russian novelist

Elizabeth of Hungary. *See* Saints

Federer, Heinrich (1866–1928), Swiss Catholic priest, novelist

Fontane, Theodor (1819–1898), German novelist, poet

Francis de Sales. *See* Saints

Frankl, Viktor E. (1905–1997), Austrian psychiatrist, Holocaust survivor

Goethe, Johann Wolfgang von (1749–1832), Classical era novelist, poet

Gordan, Paulus, OSB (1911–1999): né Günther Gordan, German Jewish Catholic convert, monk at the Benedictine Archabbey of Beuron, Germany, Catholic priest, friend of Ida Görres. Letters Görres wrote to Gordon were published after her death. (Görres. "*Wirklich die neue Phönixgestalt?*")

Görres, Albert (1918–1996), psychologist, brother-in-law of Ida Görres

Görres, Carl-Josef (1905–1973), husband of Ida Görres

Guardini, Romano (1885–1968), German Catholic priest, a leader of the Catholic Youth Movement in which Ida Görres played an active role

Häring, Bernhard, CSsR (1912–1998), German Catholic priest

Heloise (c 1101–c 1164), French nun, famous for her correspondence and relationship with Peter Abelard; *see also* Abelard

Hotz, Robert, SJ (1935– 2021), Swiss Catholic priest, and from 1971 to 1989 editor of the Swiss Jesuit publication *Orientierung*

Ivo of Chartres. *See* Saints

Joseph. *See* Saints.

Karl Marx (1818–1883), German philosopher

Kierkegaard, Søren (1813–1855), Danish philosopher

Lewis, C. S. (1898–1963), English Anglican author, he and Görres corresponded briefly

Louis (Ludwig) IV (1200–1227), Landgrave of Thuringia, husband of St. Elizabeth of Hungary; *see also* Elizabeth of Hungary

de Lubac, Henri, SJ (1896–1991), French Catholic priest, cardinal 1983–1991

Lucretia (d. 510 BC), Roman noblewoman whose suicide after being raped is associated with the events that led to the founding of the Roman Republic

Luther, Martin (1483–1546), Catholic priest, German catalyst of the Protestant Reformation, founder of Lutheranism

Mary. *See* Saints.

Maximilian I (1459–1519), Emperor of the Holy Roman Empire, husband of Mary of Burgundy

Maximos IV Sayegh (1878–1967), Cardinal Patriarch (Melkite Greek rite) of Antioch, participant at the Second Vatican Council

Montini. *See* Popes

Newman, John Henry. *See* Saints

Nicholas I. *See* Popes

Nicholas of Flüe. *See* Saints

Nietzsche, Friedrich (1844–1900), German philosopher

Novalis (1772–1801), early Romantic era German author, né Georg Philipp Friedrich Freiherr von Hardenberg

Paul VI. *See* Popes

Péguy, Charles (1873–1914), French Catholic poet, essayist

Pieper, Josef (1904–1997), German Catholic philosopher

Pius XII. *See* Popes

Popes, with years of papacy

Alexander III (1159–1181), oversaw the Third Council of the Lateran including its strengthening of canon law regarding sexual morality

Benedict XVI (2005–2013), né Joseph Ratzinger, corresponded with Görres from the 1960s until her death, delivered the eulogy at her funeral in 1971

Pope John XXIII (1958–1963), saint, convened the Second Vatican Council

Nicholas I (858–867), saint, also known as Nicholas the Great, known for his support of the indissolubility of marriage, including for royalty

Paul VI (1963–1978), saint, author of the encyclical *Humanae vitae*

Pius XII (1939–1953), saint, some of his canon law reforms dealt with marriage Saints

Rahner, Hugo, SJ (1900–1968), German Catholic priest and theologian

Rahner, Karl, SJ (1904–1984), German Catholic priest and theologian

Ratzinger, Joseph. *See* Popes

Rosenstock–Huessy, Eugen (1888–1973), German Jewish historian and social philosopher, convert to Lutheranism, emigre to the United States

Saints

Alexius (fourth century); *see* Section 62

Aquinas, Thomas, OP (1225–1274), Catholic priest, Doctor of the Church

Augustine (354–430), Catholic priest, theologian, Bishop of Hippo

Bernard of Clairvaux, Saint (1090–1153), abbot, a leading figure in Benedictine monastic revival

Elizabeth of Hungary (1207–1231), Hungarian princess with a deep commitment to helping the poor; betrothed to Louis IV in infancy; theirs became a loving marriage; *see also* Louis IV

Francis de Sales (1567–1622), Bishop of Geneva, Doctor of the Church

Ivo of Chartres (1040–1115), known for his work in canon law, Bishop of Chartres

Joseph (?–ca. 18 or 19 AD), father of Jesus, husband of St. Mary

Joseph II (1741–1790), Holy Roman Emperor, Hapsburg Emperor, promoter of Enlightenment rationalism

Mary (ca. 20 BC–ca. after 40 AD), mother of Jesus, wife of St. Joseph

Mary of Burgundy (1457–1482), duchess, wife of Emperor Maximilian I

Newman, John Henry (1801–1890), English Catholic convert, priest, cardinal

Nicholas of Flüe (1417–1487), Swiss ascetic, also known as Brother Klaus

Paul (ca. 5 to ca. 64/65), Apostle

Spengler, Oswald (1880–1936), German historian and philosopher of history

Stein, Charlotte von (1742–1827), lady-in-waiting at the court of Weimar, a friend of Johann Wolfgang Goethe

Stifter, Adalbert (1805–1868), Austrian novelist and short story writer

Stolz, Alban (1808–1883), German Catholic priest, popular author

Thibon, Gustave (1903–2001), French philosopher, convert to Catholicism, friend of Simone Weil

Undset, Sigrid (1882– 1949), Norwegian novelist, Catholic convert, recipient of the Nobel Prize for Literature in 1928

Unger, Joseph (1828–1913), Austrian legal scholar, author of a book in 1910 on legal issues, including when priests and monks seek to marry

Volk, Hermann (1903–1988), German Catholic priest; in 1970, while he was Bishop of Mainz (1962 to 1982), he nominated Görres to be a delegate at the Synod of Wurzburg in 1971

Weil, Simone (1909–1943), French philosopher, friend of Gustave Thibon

Weizsäcker, Carl Heinrich von (1822–1899), German Lutheran theologian, a translator of the New Testament

Wendland, Heinz-Dietrich (1900–1992), German Lutheran theologian

Zoghby, Elias (1912–2008), Melkite Greek Catholic Archbishop of Baalbek (1968–1988), participant in the Second Vatican Council

STUDY GUIDE

by Jennifer S. Bryson

The questions in this study guide are for book clubs, the classroom, and personal reflection.

Special thanks to Stephen Behnke, Ana Botelho, Kent Hill, Alex Lessard, and Richard Whitekettle for their assistance in trial use of this study guide.

The numbers in parentheses refer to the section numbers in the book.

1. What is the meaning of the Latin word *gens*? (See introduction by Bieler.)

2. Görres draws attention to the interrelated nature of the facets of the "conflict" in which the "freedom fighters" are engaged. (5–6)

2A. What does Görres identify as "the same deep root" of these aspirations? (6)

2B. How does this "same deep root" relate to a general hostility to authority? (6)

2C. Why, in Görres's view, is it "inevitable" that the Church would be included in this hostility to authority? (6)

3. What is the concept of "inverted envy" identified by Richard Coudenhove-Kalegi? (10)

3A. What relation does Görres see between "inverted envy" and the efforts of some Catholics to overturn the Church's teaching on marriage? (10–11)

4. Görres notes four "focal points" of a "framework," from which "marriage which is soluble and repeatable as humans see fit not only fits seamlessly, but it grows out of it." (13)

4A. Identify these four "focal points."

4B. Describe an example of how you have seen any of these four "focal points" undermine acknowledging the indissolubility of marriage.

4C. Share any "focal points" that you would add to or subtract from this "framework."

5. Identify the set of two propositions that Görres argues fundamentally undermine "the question of commitment to duration" in marriage. (15)

5A. Why does she maintain that these two propositions fundamentally undermine "the question of commitment to duration" in marriage? (15)

5B. Why does Görres maintain that this set of propositions reveals "which *basic concept* of marriage we are actually talking about" (16–17)?

6. What does Görres see as the weakness in the assertion by Hotz that "marriage is indissoluble *insofar as* it is constituted by love"? (19)

7. The advocates for allowing divorce and remarriage use the label "serial-marriage" (19). Why does Görres call this "serial polygamy" (5)?

8. What does Görres diagnose as "the core problem" at the center of the modern debates about marriage? (22)

9. "Animals," writes Görres, "are acquainted with packs and flocks, not generations." (25) How do "generations" differ from "packs and flocks"? (24, 25)

10. According to Görres: "The couple needs the *covenant* to carry out the mission of kinship." In what ways is "this, too . . . a specifically human element"? (26)

11. Görres writes: "For the covenant of marriage, sympathy, respect, appreciation, benevolence, and trust would suffice. Lifelong companionship should establish integration." (27) How does this differ from how love is portrayed in many if not most popular films and songs?

12. How does Görres describe the relationship of each of the following to marriage?

12A. eros/erotic attraction (27, 30, 31, 32, 41, 42, 45, et al.)

12B. *amicitia* (friendship, amicable bond)/fondness (27, 32, 46, et al.).

13. Why does Görres assert that "it is a *fable convenue* (a common fable) *simply to conflate partner-marriage and love-marriage*"? (37)

14. According to Görres, "Covenant, law, and grace" bind marriage forever.

14A. How does Görres describe the relationship of this trio to love? (48)

14B. How do covenant, law, and grace "bind marriage"? (48–56 et al.)

15. Görres writes: *A marriage that is becoming—that has just become a marriage—is a marriage like the way an embryo is a human. The marriage's undeveloped state gives it as little justification for its destruction as the child's underdevelopment would be justification for abortion.* (51)

Share an example from a film or novel of a marriage that went through a difficult time—and some thought it should, therefore, have been ended—but was later able to grow.

16. Görres writes about "the way the Psalms, especially Psalm 118[/119], ceaselessly praise the law." (53) This Psalm begins, "Blessed are those whose way is blameless, who walk in the law of the Lord!" Read the entire Psalm. Share a verse from this Psalm that might help spouses orient their marriage toward permanence.

17. How does Görres describe the relationship between who God is and what marriage is? (57, 60)

18. What impact does Görres think the Church's loosening of restrictions for religious who wish to be released from vows to marry may have on how the Church's teaching on marriage is viewed? (63, 64)

19. Görres writes: *From the exaggerated pendulum swing against overemphasis of days gone by of the Sixth Commandment, the fact that today, religious proclamation in all its branches—in school, sermons, literature, and mass media—hardly dares to talk about chastity and unchastity is a calamity of unforeseeable consequences. . . . Has a young generation ever been so let down in this regard? With this, cornerstones that are indispensable for every marriage are disappearing.* (69)

19A. Which "cornerstones" of marriage do you think are disappearing or have even already disappeared from our culture today?

19B. In addition to those identified by Görres, what other "cornerstones" of marriage in the premarriage years of a person's life may help foster stable or even flourishing marriages?

20. What does Görres identify as "the most profound dimension of indissolubility"? (71)

21. What was your reaction when you read about the "abandoned, divorced woman, whose husband had succumbed to a stronger fascination after a few short years of happiness," who said, "Now I have to be faithful for two" and who "persevered in this impeccably for over forty years until his death"? (71)

22. How does Görres describe the role of the priest in a Church wedding? (75)

23. Görres notes that those advocating for divorce and remarriage in the Church point to the practices of the Orthodox and some Protestants to bolster their claim. What counterarguments does Görres present from the Orthodox and Reformed Protestants to suggest that their approaches are "not exactly applause and celebration" for divorce and remarriage? (76–77)

24. What does Görres criticize about the emerging changes in annulment practices she witnessed? (80)

25. Why does Görres argue, "Marital breakdown *is* the fruit of sin, of many, long, desired, and known, cherished and cultivated sins on at least one side." (84, 85, 87, 89, 90, 95, 96, 97, 98)

26. What are the differences between these three types of love? (85, 46)
amor complacentiae (love arising from attraction)
amor concupiscentiae (love arising from desire)

amor benevolentiae (love arising from benevolence/good will)

26A. Watch the film *The Magic of Ordinary Days* or read the book. (46, *see citation* 52.)

26A-1. Which of these three types of love inform the behavior of Olivia and the soldier who is the father of her first child?

26A.-2. Identify instances in which Ray extends *amor benevolentiae* to Olivia, and Olivia to Ray.

26A.-3. What impact does receiving *amor benevolentiae* have on Olivia? On Ray? On the relationship between Olivia and Ray?

27. Görres asks: *What about people, perhaps not few, who, through "discriminating" against sin, can still be kept away from it? Is it fair, is it brotherly, by tacit complicity, by strengthening false hopes, to rob them of the last support for their conscience and let them slide when they could still pull themselves together with healing? Should we deprive them of all courage to resist by offering the adulterous partner the bonus of a happy and rehabilitated marriage with the marriage-wrecker?* (91)

27A. How does she respond? (91–92)

27B. How would you respond?

28. Reflecting on marriage, Görres writes: *The person who knows that he has to stay in his house* *tries promptly, that is, early on, to repair small damages. The person who already has a nicer place to live in sight will neglect the first one* **on purpose** *to have sufficient reasons for moving out early.* (91)

28A. Identify specific ways a couple might behave differently on a day-to-day basis if they were to consider the "house" of their marriage a lifelong dwelling place.

29. What is the nature of the pastoral response Görres hopes for in the face of marital difficulties? (85, 100 et al.)

30. Gorres warns of problems should the Church follow the calls of some to be "merciful" and therefore allow divorce and remarriage. (93 et al.)

30A. What are some problems this could engender for:

30A-1. The individual who is, for the most part, the guilty party?

30A-2. The individual who is, for the most part, the innocent party?

30A-3. The priest or other person who advises one or both parties in the marriage to opt for "divorce" and "remarriage"?

30B. What are the implications of this path for the credibility of the Church regarding marriage as well as other realms of Church teaching? (80, 93, 101)

31. Görres writes: *People can talk past each other fruitlessly for hours if they want to pursue purely factual apologetics of an abstract "indissolubility." Instead, it is about the fact that the word "marriage," which was still a clear concept yesterday, wavers and fluctuates elusively today.* (16, *see also* Translator's Preface).

31A. Share an experience in which you realized that your understanding of marriage was inadequate, shaped more by cultural assumptions than by what the Church teaches. What happened?

31B. Identify ways for Catholics—both in how they speak as well as how they live—to communicate clearly in public what they mean by the word "marriage."

CONTRIBUTORS

Jonathan Bieler is assistant professor of patrology and systematic theology at the Pontifical John Paul II Institute for Studies on Marriage and Family of The Catholic University of America.

Dr. Bieler received his doctoral degree in theology at the University of Zürich (2017) with a dissertation in Patristics on the coherence of Maximus the Confessor's thought. He earned his MA in Thomistic theology at the Dominican House of Studies, Washington, DC, and his BA and MA in Theology from the University of Zürich.

In his work, he is striving to combine the usage of historical-critical methods with faithfulness to the Church's living tradition.

* * * * *

Jennifer S. Bryson is a fellow in the Catholic Women's Forum at the Ethics and Public Policy Center in Washington, DC.

Dr. Bryson received her doctoral degree in Greco-Arabic and Islamic studies from the Department of Near Eastern Languages and Civilizations at Yale University (2000). She earned her MA in European intellectual history from Yale 1990 and her BA in political science from Stanford University.

She learned German as a teenager while attending a Gymnasium (college-preparatory school) in Austria for a year and while studying for two semesters as an undergraduate at the Karl-Marx-University in Leipzig in the former East Germany. Her doctoral work included studying theory of translation. She translated *The Church in the Flesh* (Cluny Media, 2023) and *John Henry Newman: A Life Sacrificed* (Ignatius Press, 2024) by Ida Friederike Görres from German to English. She has published translations of essays by Görres in academic journals and has authored two book chapters on the work of Görres. She previously worked for the Department of Defense and at several think tanks.

BIBLIOGRAPHY

Anonymous. "Ade zur guten Nacht." In *Deutsche Volkslieder*, edited by Horatio Stevens White, 61. G. P. Putnam's Sons, 1892.

Anonymous. "Helreith Brynhildar." In *The Poetic Edda*. Translated by Henry Adams Bellows. The American-Scandinavian Foundation, 1923.

Anonymous. "Pionierehe im neuen Südweststaat." *Badische Zeitung*. April 19, 2003. https://www.badische-zeitung.de/pionierehe-im-neuen-suedweststaat--165351236.html?mode=in

Anonymous/Attributed to Simon Dach. "Annie of Tharaw." Translated by Henry Wadsworth Longfellow. In *Poems from the German*, 149. Selected by Helen Plotz. Thomas Y. Crowell Company, 1967.

Asmussen, Hans. *Das Geheimnis der Liebe*. Verlag Die Spur, 1964.

Augustine of Hippo. "Rule." Translated by George Lawless. In *Augustine of Hippo and His Monastic Rule*. By George Lawless. Clarendon Press, 1990, 1st ed. 1987.

Baader, Franz Xaver von. "Sätze aus der erotischen Philosophie." *Münchner Blätter für Poesie, Literatur und Kunst*. No. 127–135. Leipzig, Germany, 1828.

Batlogg, Andreas. "Zwischen Pietät und Revolution. Neuentdeckung von Ida Friederike Görres." *Stimmen der Zeit* 219, no. 12 (2001): 857–60.

Bingham, Joel Foot. *Christian Marriage*. E. P. Dutton & Company, 1900.

Bryson, Jennifer S. "The Death of Ida Görres during the Synod of Würzburg & How Pieper Learned of It from Ratzinger." Exploring Ida Görres Substack, February 27, 2025. https://exploringidagoerres.substack.com/p/the-death-of-ida-gorres-during-the.

Bryson, Jennifer S. "Leselicht: Eine unabsehbare Wechselwirkung von menschlicher und göttlicher Liebe." In *Neue Schau: Große christliche Erzählungen im 20. Jahrhundert*, edited by Hanna-Barbara Gerl-Falkovitz and Gudrun Trausmuth. *Kleine Bibliothek des Abendlandes*. Be+Be-Verlag, 2023.

Chardin, Pierre Teilhard de. *Hymne an das Ewig Weibliche, Mit einem Kommentar von Henri de Lubac*. Translated by Hans Urs von Balthasar. Johannes Verlag, 1969.

Chardin, Pierre Teilhard de. "L'Évolution de la Chasteté, février 1934." In *Les directions de l'avenir. Oeuvres de Pierre Teilhard de Chardin*. Les Éditions du Seuil, 1973.

Coudenhove-Kalergi, Richard Nicolaus Graf von. *Ethik und Hyperethik*. Verlag Der neue Geist, 1921.

Creel, Ann Howard. *The Magic of Ordinary Days*. Penguin Books, 2001.

Das Neue Testament. Translated by Carl von Weizsäcker. Verlag Mohr, 1903.

Federer, Heinrich. *Am Fenster: Jugenderinnerungen*. Grote, 1927.

Findl-Ludescher, Anna. *Stützen kann nur, was widersteht: Görres, Ida Friederike, ihr Leben und ihre Kirchenschriften*. Vol. 9, *Salzburger Theologische Studien*. Tyrolia, 1999.

Fort, Gertrud von le. *Hymns to the Church*. Translated by Margaret Chanler. Sheed & Ward, 1942.

Gerl-Falkovitz, Hanna-Barbara. "Hoffnungsvoll, Verwundet, Leidenschaftlich, Alltäglich: Ehe und Gnade im Blick von Ida Friederike Görres." In *Glaube und Kirche in Zeiten des Umbruchs, Festschrift für Josef Kreiml*, edited by Veit Neumann, Josef Spindelböck, and Sigmund Bonk. Verlag Friedrich Pustet, 2018.

Gerl-Falkovitz, Hanna-Barbara. "Introduction" (working title). *On Marriage and on Being Single* by Ida Friederike Görres. Translated by Jennifer S. Bryson. Ignatius Press, 2026 (forthcoming).

Gerl-Falkovitz, Hanna-Barbara. "Zur Einstimmung." In Ida Friederike Görres, *Von Ehe und von Einsamkeit: Ein Beitrag in Briefen*. Kairos Publications, 2012.

Gerl-Falkovitz, Hanna-Barbara. "Zwischen den Zeiten: Ein Porträt von Ida Friederike Görres (1901–1971) zu ihrem 90. Geburtstag." *Communio. Internationale Katholische Zeitschrift* 20, no. 6 (1991): 560–67.

Goethe, Johann Wolfgang von. *Berliner Ausgabe. Kunsttheoretische Schriften und Übersetzungen*, Band 18. Aufbau-Verlag, 1984.

Goethe, Johann Wolfgang von. *Elective Affinities*. Translated by David Constantine. Oxford University Press, 1994.

Goethe, Johann Wolfgang von. *Faust: Part One*. Translated by Bayard Quincy Morgan. Liberal Arts Press, 1954.

Goethe, Johann Wolfgang von. "The God and the Bayadere." In *Goethe*, 48–50. Translated by John Whaley. Everyman, 2000.

Goethe, Johann Wolfgang von. *Goethes Sprüche in Prosa: Maximen und Reflexionen*. Edited by Hermann Krüger-Westend. Insel Verlag, 1908.

Görres, Ida Friederike. *Bread Grows in Winter*. Translated by Jennifer S. Bryson. Ignatius Press (forthcoming).

Görres, Ida Friederike. "The Bride of Alexius." Translated by Jennifer S. Bryson. Working title. Unpublished.

Görres, Ida Friederike. *Broken Lights: Diaries and Letters, 1951–1959*. Translated by Barbara Wartenberg-Waldstein. Burns & Oates, 1964.

Görres, Ida Friederike. "Die Braut des Alexis." In *Die Braut des Alexis und andere Mädchengeschichten*, 261–93. Verlag Herder, 1949.

Görres, Ida Friederike. “Die Braut des Alexis.” In *Neue Schau: Große christliche Erzählungen im 20. Jahrhundert*, edited by Hanna-Barbara Gerl-Falkovitz and Gudrun Trausmuth, vol. 9, 199–222. *Kleine Bibliothek des Abendlandes*. Be+Be-Verlag, 2023.

Görres, Ida Friederike. “The Bride of Alexius.” Translated by Jennifer S. Bryson. Unpublished.

Görres, Ida Friederike. *The Church in the Flesh*. Translated by Jennifer S. Bryson. Cluny Media, 2023.

Görres, Ida Friederike. “Die Erfindung der Frau: Zu Simone de Beauvoirs Le Deuxième Sexe.” *Wort und Wahrheit: Monatsschrift für Religion und Kultur* 6, no. 1 (1951): 58–63.

Görres, Ida Friederike. “Das Geheimnis ist Groß.” In *Frankfurter Ehebriefe*, edited by Ferdinand Krenzer, Chapter 9, 1–12. Lahn-Verlag, 1966.

Görres, Ida Friederike. *Die leibhaftige Kirche: Gespräch unter Laien*. Johannes Verlag, 1994.

Görres, Ida Friederike. “Marriage: This Is a Great Mystery.” Translated by Jennifer S. Bryson. Working title. Unpublished.

Görres, Ida Friederike. “Die Mischehe: Erwägungen über einige Grundlagen ihrer Neuordnung.” In *Be-Denkliches: über die Mischehe und anderes Zeitgespräch*. Verlag Ludwig Auer, 1966.

Görres, Ida Friederike. “Die Mischehe: Erwägungen über einige Grundlagen ihrer Neuordnung.” In *Wort und Wahrheit* 20, no. 5 (May 1965): 342–56.

Görres, Ida Friederike. “Einige Überlegungen zur Mischehe.” In *Be-Denkliches: über die Mischehe und anderes Zeitgespräch*, 39–55. Auer, 1966.

Görres, Ida Friederike. “Einige Überlegungen zur Mischehe.” In *Ehe* 1, no. 1 (1964).

Görres, Ida Friederike. “Geleitwort.” In *Kleiner Kompaß für Eheleute*, by Thomas Gilby, 7–12. Translated by Elisabeth Maurer. Herder, 1956.

Görres, Ida Friederike. *John Henry Newman: A Life Sacrificed.* Translated by Jennifer S. Bryson. Ignatius Press, 2024.

Görres, Ida Friederike. "Marriage in a Nutshell—or Not," Preface to *Kleiner Kompaß für Eheleute*. Translated by Jennifer S. Bryson. Working title. Unpublished.

Görres, Ida Friederike. "Mixed-Marriage: Considerations on Some Basic Principles for Reassessing Mixed-Marriage." Translated by Jennifer S. Bryson. Working title. Unpublished.

Görres, Ida Friederike. "Neues über die Liebe? Asmussen, Hans, 'Das Geheimnis der Liebe.'" *Der Christliche Sonntag* 15, no. 30 (1963): 237–38.

Görres, Ida Friederike. *Nocturnen: Tagebuch und Aufzeichnungen.* Verlag Josef Knecht, 1949.

Görres, Ida Friederike. *On Marriage and on Being Single* (working title). Translated by Jennifer S. Bryson. Ignatius Press, 2026 (forthcoming).

Görres, Ida Friederike. "Our Image of Christ." In *Bread Grows in Winter*. Translated by Jennifer S. Bryson. Ignatius Press (forthcoming).

Görres, Ida Friederike. "'Satanic,' 'An Atheistic Doctrine of Woman': A Review of Simone de Beauvoir's *The Second Sex* (1951)." Translated by Jan C. Bentz and Jennifer S. Bryson. *Interpretation: A Journal of Political Philosophy* 49, no. 3 (2023): 411–22.

Görres, Ida Friederike. "Some Thoughts Regarding Mixed Marriage." Translated by Jennifer S. Bryson. Working Title. Unpublished.

Görres, Ida Friederike. "Trusting the Church: A Lecture." In *Bread Grows in Winter.* Translated by Jennifer S. Bryson. Ignatius Press (forthcoming).

Görres, Ida Friederike, ed. "Überlegungen zur künstlichen Menschenerzeugung." In *Der karierte Christ und andere Glossen und Beiträge*, 66–77. Knecht Verlag, 1966.

Görres, Ida Friederike. *Von Ehe und von Einsamkeit: Ein Beitrag in Briefen.* Mit Einer Einstimmung von Hanna-Barbara Gerl-Falkovitz. Kairos Publications, 2012.

Görres, Ida Friederike. "Wiederverheiratung Geschiedener?" *Theologisches*, no. 24 (1972): 107–10. [This article consists of excerpts from Görres's book *Was Ehe auf immer bindet*, compiled by the journal *Theologisches*.]

Görres, Ida Friederike. *"Wirklich die neue Phönixgestalt?" Über Kirche und Konzil; Unbekannte Briefe 1962–1971 von Görres, Ida Friederike an Paulus Gordan.* Edited by Hanna-Barbara Gerl-Falkovitz. Be+Be Verlag, 2015.

Görres, Ida Friederike. *Zwischen den Zeiten: Aus meinen Tagebüchern 1951 bis 1959*. Walter Verlag, 1960.

Guardini, Romano. "Das Erwachen der Kirche in der Seele." *Hochland* 19 (1922): 257–67.

Guardini, Romano. *Der Mensch und der Glaube: Versuche über die religiöse Existenz in Dostojewskijs großen Romanen*. Hegner, 1932.

Guardini, Romano. *The Lord*. Translated by Elinor Castendyk Briefs. Henry Regnery, 1954.

Hotz, Robert. "Wiederverheiratung Geschiedener in der Kirche?" *Orientierung* 34, no. 20 (October 1970): 211–18. http://www.orientierung.ch.

Institut de droit canonique. "Le Lien Matrimonial: Colloque organisé à l'occasion du cinquantenaire de l'Institut de droit canonique de l'Université de Strasbourg." *Revue de Droit Canonique* 21, no. 1–4. Université de Strasbourg, 1971.

International Commission on English in the Liturgy (ICEL) Secretariat. *The Order of Celebrating Matrimony 2013*. ICEL, 2020. https://svdpks.org/wp-content/uploads/2020/07/Selections-for-Marriage-Rite.pdf

Kierkegaard, Søren. *For Self-Examination: Judge for Yourself!* Translated by Howard V. Hong and Edna H. Hong. Princeton University Press, 1990.

Kleinert, Michael. *Es wächst viel Brot in der Winternacht: Theologische Grundlinien im Werk von Ida Friederike Görres*. Vol. 36, *Studien zur systematischen und spirituellen Theologie*. Echter, 2002.

Lapide, Cornelius a. *Commentary on Genesis 1–3*. Translated by Craig Toth. Kolbe Center for the Study of Creation, 2019.

Lewis, C. S. *The Four Loves*. Harcourt Brace, 1960.

Lubac, Henri de. *The Eternal Feminine: A Study on the Poem by Teilhard de Chardin, Followed by Teilhard and the Problems of Today*. Translated by René Hague. Harper & Row, 1971.

Luther, Martin. "A Sermon on the Estate of Marriage." Translated by A.T.W. Steinhaeuser. In *Martin Luther's Basic Theological Writings*. Edited by Timothy F. Lull and William R. Russell, 387–91. Fortress Press, 2012.

Luther, Martin. "The Babylonian Captivity of the Church." Translated by A.T.W. Steinhaeuser. In *Three Treatises*. Muhlenberg Press, 1943.

Marx, Karl. "The Divorce Bill" (*Rheinische Zeitung* no. 353, December 19, 1842). In *Karl Marx Friedrich Engels Collected Works* Vol. 1, 307–10. Lawrence & Wishart, 1975.

Maximos, Patriarch of Antioch. *The Melkite Church at the Council*. Translated by Anonymous. Newton, Massachusetts: Eparchy of Newton: Sophia Press, 2014. https://melkite.org /faith/ faith-worship/chapter-15

McDonald, Peter. *The Oxford Dictionary of Medical Quotations*. Oxford University Press, 2004.

Michael, Johannes Petrus. "Ehe." In *Lexikon für Theologie und Kirche*. Edited by Joseph Höffner and Karl Rahner, 3:675–99. Verlag Herder, 1959.

Morris, Desmond. *Der nackte Affe*. Translated by Fritz Bolle. Droemer Knaur, 1973. First edition 1968.

Morris, Desmond. *The Naked Ape. A Zoologist's Study of the Human Animal*. McGraw-Hill, 1967.

Newman, John Henry. *The Idea of a University*. Longmans, Green and Co., 1905. Newmanreader.org.

Newman, John Henry. *Lectures on the Prophetical Office of the Church*. In *Via Media*, vol. 1. Longmans, Green and Co., 1901.

Newman, John Henry. "On the Introduction of Rationalistic Principles into Revealed Religion, (Tract No. 73, Ad Scholas)." In *Essays Critical & Historical* 1:30–48. Longmans, Green and Co., 1907. Newmanreader.org.

Nietzsche, Friedrich. *On the Genealogy of Morals*. Translated by Horace B. Samuel. T.N. Foulis, 1913.

Nietzsche, Friedrich. *Thus Spoke Zarathustra*. Translated by Walter Kaufmann. Penguin Books, 1978.

Novalis. *Pollen and Fragments: Selected Poetry and Prose of Novalis*. Translated by Arthur Versluis. Phanes Press, 1989.

Péguy, Charles. *The Portal of the Mystery of Hope*. Translated by David Louis Schindler Jr. Eerdmans, 2005.

Pieper, Josef. "Temperance." In *The Four Cardinal Virtues*, 143–206. Translated by Daniel F. Coogan. University of Notre Dame Press, 1966.

Rahner, Hugo. *Symbole der Kirche: Die Ekklesiologie der Väter*. Otto Müller Verlag, 1964.

Rahner, Karl. "Die Zukunft der Orden in Welt und Kirche von heute." *Geist und Leben* 43 (1970): 338–54.

Ratzinger, Joseph. Ratzinger, Joseph. "Eulogy for Ida Friederike Görres." *In Bread Grows in Winter* by Ida Friederike Görres, translated by Jennifer S. Bryson. Ignatius Press (forthcoming).

Ratzinger, Joseph. "Zur Theologie der Ehe." In *Joseph Ratzinger Gesammelte Schriften*, Verlag Herder. 4:565–92.

Rosenstock-Huessy, Eugen. *Soziologie: Die Übermacht der Räume*, Vol. 1. W. Kohlhammer Verlag, 1956.

Rosenstock-Huessy, Eugen. *Soziologie: Die Vollzahl der Zeiten*, Vol. 2. W. Kohlhammer Verlag, 1958.

Sales, Francis de. *Introduction to the Devout Life*. Translated by John K. Ryan. Image Books, 1989.

Scheffczyk, Leo. "Ein Nachwort." In *Die leibhaftige Kirche: Gespräch unter Laien*, 281–85. By Ida Friederike Görres. Johannes Verlag, 1994.

Scheffczyk, Leo. "Eucharistie und Ehesakrament: Dogmatische Grundlegungen in der Frage nach der Zulassung geschiedener Wiederverheirateter zur Eucharistie." *Münchener Theologische Zeitschrift* 27, no. 4 (1976): 351–75.

Scheffczyk, Leo. "Foreword." In *The Church in the Flesh*. By Ida Friederike Görres. Translated by Jennifer S. Bryson. Cluny Media, 2023.

Shields, Brent, dir. "The Magic of Ordinary Days." (Empire Pictures and Hallmark Hall of Fame Productions, 2005). TV Movie.

Spengler, Oswald. *Der Untergang des Abendlandes*, Vol 2. Oskar Beck, 1922.

Sternberger, Adolf ("Dolf"), Gerhard Storz, and W. E. Suskind, eds. *Aus dem Wörterbuch des Unmenschen*. Claassen, 1957.

Stifter, Adalbert. *Der Waldgänger*. Nicolai, 2015 (first edition 1847).

Stolz, Alban. *Spanisches für die gebildete Welt*. 4th ed. Herder'sche Verlagshandlung, 1859.

Thibon, Gustave. *Love at the Crossroads*. Translated by Reginald Trevett and S. F. L. Tye. Burns and Oates, 1964.

Undset, Sigrid. *Kristin Lavransdatter: A Trilogy*. Translated by Charles Archer and J. S. Scott. Alfred A. Knopf, 1939.

Undset, Sigrid. *The Master of Hestviken: A Tetralogy*. Translated by Arthur G. Chater. Alfred A. Knopf, 1952.

Ungar, Joseph. *Priesterehen und Mönchsehen. Rechtliche Natur der Scheidung von Tisch und Bett. Zwei Abhandlungen aus dem österreichischen Recht*. Verlag Gustav Fischer, 1910.

Unkel, Karl. *Berthold von Regensburg*. J. P. Bachem, 1882.

Vatican Council II. *Pastoral Constitution on the Church in the Modern World: Gaudium et Spes*. Promulgated by His Holiness Pope Paul VI. December 7, 1965.

Wayne, T. G. *Morals and Marriage*. Longmans, Green and Co., 1936.

Wendland, Heinz-Dietrich. *Botschaft an die soziale Welt: Beiträge zur christlichen Sozialethik der Gegenwart*. Im Furche Verlag, 1959.

Wendland, Heinz-Dietrich. "Zur Theologie der Sexualität und der Ehe." In *Theologie der Ehe: Veröffentlichung des ökumenischen Arbeitskreises Evangelischer und Katholischer Theologen*, edited by Gerhard Krems and Reinhard Mumm. Friedrich Pustet, 1969.

Wight, Orlando Williams, Peter Abelard, Héloïse, Alphonse de Lamartine. *Lives and Letters of Abelard and Heloise*. M. Doolady, 1861.

INDEX OF BIBLICAL REFERENCES

OLD TESTAMENT

NEW TESTAMENT

INDEX

A

B

C

D

E

F

G

H

I

L

M

N

O

P

R

S

T

U

V

W

Y

Z

BACK COVER, 1971 EDITION

The back cover of the German edition of *What Binds Marriage Forever* (1971):

Ida Friederike Görres was an intrepid voice "in a desert of conformism or embarrassed silence"* (J. Ratzinger). She completed the manuscript of this "unsystematic reflection on the indissolubility of marriage" eight days before her death. Inspired by the fulness of the Catholic faith, in a sober and, at the same time, engaging analysis of this question, which is often discussed passionately today, she seeks to bring clarity to the reality of human life, to do justice to human distress, and to shed light on possible trends. Since she places the problem in the context of our current situation, the reader gains insights far beyond the immediate topic.

* Joseph Ratzinger, "Eulogy for Ida Friederike Görres."